THE LILY OF THE VALLEY

Borgo Press Books Translated by FRANK J. MORLOCK

Anna Karenina: A Play in Five Acts, by Edmond Guiraud, from the Novel by Leo Tolstoy

Anthony: A Play in Five Acts, by Alexandre Dumas, Père

The Children of Captain Grant: A Play in Five Acts, by Jules Verne and Adolphe d'Ennery

Crime and Punishment: A Play in Three Acts, by Frank J. Morlock, from the Novel by Fyodor Dostoyevsky

Don Quixote: A Play in Three Acts, by Victorien Sardou, from the Novel by Miguel de Cervantes Saavedra

Falstaff: A Play in Four Acts, by William Shakespeare, John Dennis, William Kendrick, and Frank J. Morlock

Jesus of Nazareth: A Play in Three Acts, by Paul Demasy

Joan of Arc: A Play in Five Acts, by Charles Desnoyer

The Lily of the Valley: A Play in Five Acts, by Théodore Barrière and Arthur de Beauplan, from the Novel by Honoré de Balzac

Michael Strogoff: A Play in Five Acts, by Adolphe d'Ennery and Jules Verne

The Mysteries of Paris: A Play in Five Acts, by Eugène Sue and Prosper Dinaux

Peau de Chagrin: A Play in Five Acts, by Louis Judicis, from the Novel by Honoré de Balzac

A Raw Youth: A Play in Five Acts, by Frank J. Morlock, from the Novel by Fyodor Dostoyevsky

Richard Darlington: A Play in Three Acts, by Alexandre Dumas, Père

The San Felice: A Play in Five Acts, by Maurice Drack, from the Novel by Alexander Dumas, Père

Shylock, the Merchant of Venice: A Play in Three Acts, by Alfred de Vigny

The Voyage Through the Impossible: A Play in Three Acts, by Adolphe d'Ennery and Jules Verne

William Shakespeare: A Play in Six Acts, by Ferdinand Dugué

THE LILY OF THE VALLEY

A PLAY IN FIVE ACTS

by

THÉODORE BARRIÈRE
& ARTHUR DE BEAUPLAN

Translated and Adapted by Frank J. Morlock

From the Novel by Honoré de Balzac

THE BORGO PRESS

An Imprint of Wildside Press LLC

MMIX

www.wildsidebooks.com

FIRST WILDSIDE EDITION

CONTENTS

DEDICATION

To Heide Herr, for her help in providing me with texts to translate.

ABOUT FRANK J. MORLOCK

FRANK J. MORLOCK has written and translated many plays since retiring from the legal profession in 1992. His translations have also appeared on Project Gutenberg, the Alexandre Dumas Père web page, Literature in the Age of Napoléon, Infinite Artistries.com, and Munsey's (formerly Blackmask). In 2006 he received an award from the North American Jules Verne Society for his translations of Verne's plays. He lives and works in México.

CAST OF CHARACTERS

Count de Mortsauf
Félix
de Vandenesse
Chessel
De Cerny
De Rouvières
Henriette, Countess de Mortsauf
Lady Arabella Dudley
Duchess de Lenoncourt, Henriette's mother
Emmeline, Chessel's daughter
Doctor Origet
Manette, the Count's maid

Six men, five women

ACT I

An elegant boudoir opening on very well-lit salons. Doors in the back. To the left, a chimney. In front of the chimney, a table for whist placed obliquely to the right. Facing the chimney, a console with a vase of flowers and ice. Near the console two arm chairs facing the audience.

At rise, De Cerny is at the game table where there are only three players. Whist with a dead hand. Chessel is standing in their midst. Guests can be seen circulating in the salons.

Cerny (addressing his partner as he reveals his cards)
I assure you, sir, you've played against all the rules.

Chessel (holding a fan in his hand)
Ah, there's my friend de Cerny who starts preaching over a game of whist.

Cerny (to his partner)
What! I offer you a spade and you play hearts.

Partner
That's all I've got!

Chessel (aside)
That's a reason.

(looking at the fan he holds in his hands)

My, this is a pretty fan!

Rouvières (entering from the left and speaking to someone who follows him)
What—why certainly, sir. Be convinced. Be convinced
that the local roads in this area will have all my sympathy.

Chessel (noticing him)
Ah, now here's that dear fellow Rouvières at grips with an
influential elector!

Cerny (as they give cards to Rouvières)
Bravo, my dear candidate, bravo! And how's your candi-
dacy going? Voices abound, right? Do you know, your
ball is charming! You do things admirably!

Rouvières
Yes, isn't it? It's gallant, it's nice! Flowers everywhere,
torrents of syrup and heaps of ices! Even men. I recommended no one pass them their plates over their heads.

Chessel
Which has two inconveniences. They can't take any and
they can receive it.

Cerny
Ah, this soiree will be epoch making. They will talk of it a
long while in our good city of Tours as the most beautiful
ball in the year of Grace 1816.

Rouvières
Why, yes, I hope so.

(going to Chessel) Ah, now, my dear deputy. And this
charming young man your ravishing granddaughter pre-
sented to me—what's become of him? I don't see him!

Chessel
Mr. de Vandenesse—I confided him to the care of Lady Arabella Dudley.

Cerny (distracted by this name)
Huh?

Rouvières
Ah, that delicious Englishwoman.

Cerny (aside)
They're speaking of Lady Arabella.

Chessel (to Rouvières)
She will launch him.

Rouvières (laughing)
Watch out!

(looking to the back with Chessel) But see, what a charming company. All the men are distinguished, all the women are pretty.

Cerny (at his seat)
That dear Rouvières, always optimistic.

Chessel
It's an illness. He sees everything through rose-colored glasses.

Rouvières
By the way, have you seen my wife?

Chessel (aside, laughing)
She, by the way, is lucky.

Rouvières
Isn't she magnificent? She's covered with diamonds!

Chessel
Oh, she's splendid! From a distance you'd say a meadow lark.

Rouvières
Ah! Ah! Very pretty, without goodbyes!

Chessel (calling to him)
Ah, say, if you see my daughter, my little Emmeline, send her to me.

(pointing to the salon) I don't want to risk myself in that pit!

Rouvières
Very well! Au revoir!

(Rouvières goes out.)

Cerny (laughing, to Chessel who comes forward)
Ah, ah, ah! That poor Rouvières. It's astonishing, my word, that he can be ridiculous to that degree and not notice anything.

Chessel
Ah! Ah! You think so? That happens all the time. Ah, ah! That happens.

Emmeline (entering)
You were asking for me?

Chessel
Yes, I wanted to know what had become of you.

Emmeline
And I—what you are doing? Are you getting bored?

Chessel
Sufficiently. And you, are you amusing yourself?

Emmeline
Enormously. I haven't missed a single dance and I haven't met any completely clumsy dancers.

Chessel
Completely?

Emmeline
Oh, cruelly! Imagine the third one—he told me it was really hot and escorted me back to my seat where the currents of air are dangerous.

Chessel
Little ingrate. The wretch must have tried enormously hard to do that!

Emmeline
Ah! You don't know? I invited Félix for the first dance.

(music from the hall is heard)

But, despite him, he didn't dare. I think that's the waltz.

Chessel
Let me escort you back.

Emmeline
No. Don't come, it's too hot for you, and then, you can't walk very fast. Bye.

(Emmeline goes out. Arabella enters seemingly in search of someone.)

Chessel (watching Emmeline leave)
Dear little angel, go.

(coming back, breaking the fan he still has in his hands)

Ahh! Broke it!

Cerny (aside)
Arabella! She's in quest of me, let's not see anything.

Chessel (going to Arabella)
Ah. You're looking for someone or something?

Arabella (preoccupied)
Yes, that is to say, I lost something and I'm looking for something. Ah, dear sir, that's my fan you've got there.

Chessel
Oh, pardon. I just broke it. A minute sooner and you would have saved its life.

Arabella
And I am coming to authenticate the deceased—I thank you.

Cerny (aside)
Pretext. She's coming for me.

Arabella
My poor fan!

Chessel
I thought it belonged to the Duchess.

Arabella
The excuse is clever.

(pointing to the broken fan)

If I returned the young man you confided to me in this condition?

Chessel
Ah, indeed. What's become of dear Félix?

Arabella
This is the third time he's escaped me. He's like a mad man, he hurls himself into quadrilles, he crosses through the midst of the most intrepid dancers, he looks impudently and innocently at the women like curious birds he's never seen before. The music carries him away. The lights attract him. He seems like a butterfly who is going to burn himself up in the flame of the candles.

Chessel
To suddenly pass from the bridge of a warship into the midst of two hundred people who have the air of dancing, smiling and amusing themselves—to pass from the music of the waves and winds to the vulgar noises of the orchestra that carry you off. He's got some right to lose his mind.

Arabella
Also, I pardon him—and with all my heart. Oh! He has a wild nature which is very amusing. As for me, I love him very much.

Chessel
Already?

Arabella
Yes, you know. On his table are the most savory, civilized fruits, and he tastes them with a really dark sip and really greater pleasure than he gleaned in a hedgerow tearing his hands.

Chessel
You are very blunt.

Arabella
It's my only quality. But you, dear sir, you are bad.

Chessel
That's my only defect.

Cerny (aside)
I won't even raise my eyes.

(aloud) We have the luck—

Arabella (noticing Cerny)
Ah! Heavens, it's you? Hello, dear—

Cerny
Milady!

(aside) She's got me.

Arabella (to Chessel)
As for the rest, I will tell you I am extremely displeased with him, your little sea wolf. He's already told me he loves blue eyes and mine are black, blond hair and mine's nut brown. Still, he hasn't yet said four words to me without leveling twenty impertinent compliments.

Chessel
And you haven't offered him his choice of weapons?

Arabella
If he was a woman, right.

(disdainfully) But a man! He'd let himself be killed, it would be truly shameful.

(looking at Cerny's cards) Hearts! Mr. Cerny, hearts. You have a full suit—you must play them.

Cerny (aside)
I understand.

Arabella (to Rouvières who has just entered)
Ah, my dear sir. I need your arm. If you like, we will go on a crusade in search of the infidel.

Rouvières
Ah! Ah! Very pretty. Charming.

Chessel
(coming to Arabella) Rouvières, what are you laughing about?

Rouvières (embarrassed)
Me? Why, I was laughing—I was laughing—

Chessel (low to Arabella)
Ah, very well. He didn't hear, it's in confidence.

Arabella
(low) It's the official laugh of the candidate.

Rouvières (leaving with Arabella)
Have you seen my wife, milady?

Arabella
No. I haven't yet had that honor.

Rouvières
Oh! She's magnificent tonight. She's covered with diamonds.

(Arabella and Rouvières disappear.)

Cerny (aside)
Bravo! She's leaving furious.

A Player (giving money to Cerny)
Sir, here are your winnings.

Cerny (rising and passing to leave)
A thousand thanks. Well! In total I lost ten crowns.

Chessel (to gamblers)
You must never believe half of what he says.

Cerny (laughing)
I haven't the luck of Mr. Chessel. Lucky man, par excellence.

Chessel
It's true. Everything succeeds for me. I have a charming daughter who preaches to me and prevents me from doing too many stupid things—a handsome fortune which prevents too many debts—a position in the State which prevents me from being malcontented—and finally, an excellent constitution which prevents me from being ill. My word of honor I am very satisfied with my person. And

you, with yours?

Cerny
Enchanted.

Chessel
You're right, indulgence is a virtue!

(The players laugh and leave.)

Cerny (mysteriously)
Say, did you see just now how cautiously I played?

Chessel
At whist?

Cerny
No, with her.

Chessel
Who's "her"?

Cerny
Lady Arabella Dudley.

Chessel
Ah, you played—I don't understand.

Cerny
What, you didn't understand her trick?

Chessel
No.

Cerny
She came here just now for me.

Chessel
Not possible!

Cerny
And did you notice all the advances she made me?

Chessel
My word, no!

Cerny
And her last advice—hearts! Hearts! Play hearts, Mr. Cerny. You've got them in your hand, you must lay them out, you must play them. Do you understand?

Chessel
What—you think?

Cerny
I am sure of it.

Chessel
And to the summons, that's how you will respond?

Cerny
It's on purpose. It's a calculation, it's a system. Lady Arabella, she's eccentricity par excellence. She's eccentricity personified—and Lady Arabella, loved, surrounded, adulated by all everywhere—detests people who play court to her. She distinguishes only those who do not pay attention to her. That stings her, that irritates her.

Chessel
Yes, it's new fruit. It's the wild berry of the hedgerow.

Cerny (who doesn't understand)
Huh?

Chessel
No, nothing. Go on!

Cerny
Well, now that's the main key to my tactics. She runs after me, I flee her. She looks at me, I turn away my eyes. She speaks to me, I hardly reply.

Chessel
Take care, take care, she could indeed release herself from your severity and I think that this evening she's very much occupied with my friend Félix de Vandenesse.

Cerny
Who's that? That young sailor that you brought to the ball?

Chessel
Precisely.

Cerny
But, my good fellow, don't you see anything?

Chessel
What do you mean?

Cerny
Why, that young man is quite simply a ghost, a scarecrow. There's always someone like that who is sacrificed.

Chessel (laughing and mocking him)
Very well. I've got it. A straw man whom burns all day and who is extinguished at night.

Cerny (also laughing)
The very thing.

Chessel
Ah, indeed! Say then, and Lord Dudley, her husband?

Cerny
Oh, the husband. No one knows what's become of him. He must be in the Indies, busy studying the habits of crocodiles.

Emmeline (coming in)
Ah, father, if you knew. I am furious.

Chessel
What's wrong?

Emmeline
Félix just made me miss a dance.

Chessel
How?

Rouvières (entering with a guest)
Let's see, you want a partner? Ah! Wait. There's Mr. Chessel who's going to be on your side.

Chessel
Me?

Rouvières
Cards?

Chessel
Gladly.

(to Emmeline) You'll allow me?

Emmeline
Yes, if you don't play for too big stakes and if you follow my advice.

Chessel
Come on, that's fine. I will hold the cards.

(Chessel sits at the table.)

Emmeline
Can you believe Félix? I invited him, I waited for him—and he left me there in the tapestry, on my bench—

Chessel (joking)
That's not the way to win a name for oneself.

Cerny (bowing to Emmeline)
Miss!

Emmeline
Do you grasp that, sir? A lad we almost raised, my father and I.

Chessel
Note that he's seven years older than she is and that he's her godfather.

Emmeline
A school boy that was my father's ward in Paris and that we took out every Sunday from his prison—his college—a large dark house with iron bars. Oh! it was terrifying and when I went to see him, my heart was downhearted and he consoled me. He was really nice to me, then. But today he's a sailor, a gentleman—he treats me like a little child. He forgets me. Oh, I'm going to scold him.

Chessel
Fine!

Emmeline
No, I will pout at him.

Cerny
That will be better!

(noticing Arabella enter on Félix's arm, aside) There she is again! I was sure of it, with the scarecrow. Very well.

Emmeline (noticing Félix, low to her father)
Heavens! There he is escorting Lady Arabella. Only, I shan't speak to him. Play trumps, go on.

(Chessel starts to play.)

Chessel
Why, I don't have any.

Emmeline (without looking)
Well, play something else.

Chessel (laughing)
That's an idea!

Arabella (crosses with Félix)
Ah, Mr. Vandenesse, you love for a woman to be a woman?

Félix
Yes, Madame.

Arabella
Well, as for me, sir, I have a mania for rifles. Like a hunter

of Chamois, I can slay buck at two hundred paces. I ride a horse like an Amazon and I would be capable of winning the prize in a steeplechase against Centaurs, for no horse, however spirited it may be, can resist this hand, so delicate in appearance. Here, see, it's like steel.

(shakes his hand)

Félix (smiling)
Indeed!

Cerny (aside)
Poor young man. If he know all that is for me.

Arabella
By the way, since you are stuck here in Touraine for a month, I must give you charitable warning. If, in the evening you see a white ghost in our beautiful valley, borne by a foaming courser, crossing the thickets with her untied hair flowing in the wind of the storm, flee! For you can say it's she, and it will be me, always me.

Cerny (aside)
It's a rendezvous! I won't go!

Arabella
Why, what are you thinking about? Are you bored?

Félix (embarrassed and annoyed)
Milady—

Arabella
Wait, I return you your freedom presently. Here's Mr. Cerny who's asking me for a waltz.

Cerny
Me?

Arabella
And I grant it to him.

Cerny (aside)
She won't give up, poor little woman.

(Cerny offers his arm to Arabella.

Félix (to Emmeline)
Emmeline, isn't this the first dance you promised me?

Emmeline
No, it's the last—and you made me lose it.

Félix
Oh, my good Emmeline, I really ask your pardon for it.

Emmeline (to her father)
Do I have to forgive him?

Chessel
Yes, go on. He didn't know what he was doing.

Emmeline (giving her hand to Félix)
Here.

Arabella (on the arm of Cerny, passing near Chessel)
Be happy, my dear Chessel!

Chessel
You are leaving then, milady?

Arabella
Oh, you aren't thinking what you are saying.

(Arabella and Cerny leave.)

Emmeline (to Félix)
Félix, do you like the face of Lady Arabella? As for me, I find her really pretty.

Félix
As for me, no. There are some uglies I prefer to a beauty like that! That woman cannot have a heart.

Chessel (low to Félix, leaving the game)
On the contrary, she has too much.

Emmeline
Since peace is established, I ask you again to dance.

Servant (announcing from the back)
The Count and Countess of Mortsauf.

Emmeline
My good Henriette. I was really afraid she wouldn't come. I'm going to hug her!

Chessel
Go, my child. But try not to bring us that polar bear of a husband of hers.

Emmeline (to Félix)
Stay here. I will come find you.

(Exit Emmeline. Henriette can be seen crossing the stage with Emmeline in the distance. Chessel notices a big bouquet on a chair.)

Chessel
Heavens! Here's a bouquet that smells nice. That's odd though!

(Chessel turns the bouquet about, smelling it. Little by little he ruins it.)

Félix (aside, noticing Henriette)
O! Charming person.

(to Rouvières, who enters from the right) What's the name of that young lady who just entered?

Rouvières
She's the Countess of Mortsauf. The Count is giving her his arm.

Félix
Ah, she's married?

Rouvières
Yes, she's the daughter of the Duchess of Lenoncourt.

Félix (repeating mechanically)
Lenoncourt?

Rouvières
Yes, the Duchess of Lenoncourt—the kind, even the virtuous.

Chessel (to himself)
Huh? What's that the candidate said?

Félix
And the Count of Mortsauf?

Rouvières
An émigré. An old gentleman in the army of the Condé, virtuous, honorable, even kind!

Chessel (aside)
That's the way history is written!

Félix (very moved)
And his young wife?

Rouvières
Ah, virtuous.

Chessel (rising and leaving the now tattered bouquet on the sofa)
Kind even, it's agreed and all life is like that.

Rouvières
You'll allow me. I am going to tell them good evening.

(Rouvières goes out.)

Chessel
What the devil, my dear Félix? You address yourself to the master of the house who wants to become a deputy to obtain detailed information on influential electors in his department. Why, that's an unforgivable naivety.

(leading him to the door and seating him before him)

Look, from here it's a real magic lantern. Lady Arabella, who's seated over there is a bold coquette. She hurls epigrams which slay a rival at fifty paces. Her cavalier, Mr. de Cerny, a fool who poses eternally without anyone noticing. As for that lady, still beautiful and dressed in a stately way enthroned over there by the chimney, that's

Madame de Lenoncourt, a Duchess of the old school, as insolent as a parvenu. And her son-in-law, the Count de Mortsauf, the one who's friend to that over-desolated gentleman, he's a character turned into a man, an egoist who lives in his old Château like a snail in his shell. There's the faithful portrait of those folks, cleaned, if only for a moment, of all the theological virtues.

Félix
But the Countess of Mortsauf that Emmeline is embracing at the moment?

Chessel
Ah, that one. She's an angel, a good genius who spends her days burying her husband's absurdities to weed life's way for him.

Félix (moved)
Ah!

Chessel (moving back)
They have one child, Madeleine. A puny creature that the doctors have condemned and to whom Countess Mortsauf gives her blood and her soul. The poor mother always hangs on her lips, thinking to breathe life into her.

Félix (still looking at the Countess)
I no longer see her!

(Emmeline brings Henriette in. They are followed by the Count.)

Emmeline (to Henriette)
Come this way, my good Henriette, you will be much better.

Henriette
I wanted to greet my mother.

Count (fanning himself with his handkerchief)
Oof! How hot it is!

(The Count throws himself into an armchair.)

Emmeline
If I meet the Duchess de Lenoncourt, I will tell her you are in this boudoir.

Henriette
Yes, won't you, dear child?

(Félix has hung back contemplating them.)

Emmeline (to Félix)
Come on, Félix. This is the dance I promised you.

Félix (troubled)
Ah, yes, the dance—that's true.

Emmeline (mocking him)
The dance—that's true! What's wrong with him? Ah!

(in a low voice) You're admiring my good friend. Isn't my Henriette pretty? Do you think she has a heart?

Félix (very moved)
Yes. Yes.

Emmeline (pulling him)
Come on, come on. There won't be any more room on the dance floor.

(Emmeline leaves with Félix who turns at the last moment to look at Henriette.)

Henriette (watching Emmeline leave)
What health! What freshness!

(sighing) You are really lucky, Mr. Chessel!

Chessel (a bit embarrassed)
Yes, indeed, but—(excitedly) When she was small, she was very delicate.

Henriette (with a kind smile)
Ah! what hope!

Chessel
Yes.

(aside) Poor woman! It's not true, Emmeline was rosy and chubby like a cherubim.

(aloud) Well, and you, my dear neighbor, how is it going with you?

Count
Badly.

Henriette
Are you ill, my friend?

Count
What a question!

(shrugging his shoulders)

You can see plainly. I was suffocating in there—and I'm

freezing in here.

(The Duchess enters with Rouvières.)

Duchess
Look around, my dear Rouvières, pester yourself, act, beat the drum. I've lost an enormous bouquet.

Rouvières
Then I will go look on the other side.

Duchess
(to Henriette) Ah, there you are, little one. Hello.

Henriette
I greet you, mother.

Count
Madame!

Duchess
Hello, Mr. Chessel. Stay put, son-in-law.

(to Henriette) Why, how late you are. All the same, you were really inspired. It's so bourgeois in there. It smells of Sunday on the Rue Saint-Denis.

Chessel (aside)
She's charming.

Henriette
Mother, will we be lucky enough to keep you a long while in Touraine?

Duchess
My word, no. I am only passing through. I'm staying at an

inn—like a commercial traveler. It's odious!

Henriette
You've forgotten the way here?

Duchess
On the contrary, I remembered it. A way furrowed with ruts that could hide the whole municipal council. Much obliged, but I have no inclination to break my neck to climb up to your dungeon.

Count (aside)
Dungeon!

Chessel (aside)
If the Countess has a mother's heart, she didn't get it through inheritance.

Duchess
Besides, it's not you I wanted to see, but a very pretty little out of the way castle which was for sale and that Lady Arabella just bought precisely as an apartment for me. By the way, how's your daughter?

Henriette
Alas, still very languishing.

Duchess
Really, that's a nuisance!

(to Count who, still seated, takes candies from a box) And you, Count, still languishing, too, of course?

Count (coldly)
Duchess!

Duchess (laughing)
You're still taking pills? Don't you have a doctor in one of your pockets?

Count
Jest, Madame, jest—when perhaps I don't have six months to live.

Duchess
Ha, you have the effect on me of one of those people who eternally pack their bags and never leave.

Henriette (low)
Mother!

Count (dryly)
Does that annoy you?

Duchess
As for me, it's all the same. I don't desire your death.

Chessel (aside)
She doesn't love her daughter enough for that.

(Chessel picks up the bouquet.)

Duchess (to Chessel)
Well, sir, aren't you going to say anything? You don't have spiteful things to say?

Chessel
No! I am content to think them.

Duchess
Pretext! You decline, Chessel—it's age.

Chessel
Oh, let's not speak of that, Duchess.

Duchess (laughing)
Now, there you are on the point of an impertinence!

Chessel
Perhaps—

Duchess
Well! Let yourself go, I'm not afraid of anything.

Chessel
Bah!

Duchess
Doubtless, my dear, no one is ever as old as they seem.

(noticing the bouquet in Chessel's hands) Ah, indeed! Why, God forgive me, that's my bouquet you've put in that dreadful condition.

Chessel
Oh, yes, it's true.

Duchess
You always have to destroy something or someone. My poor flowers!

Chessel (throwing a fistful of rose leaves before the Duchess)
I sow them under your feet, Duchess.

Duchess
Do you take me for a procession?

Chessel
My word, well, you are dressed like a reliquary.

Mortsauf (laughing, low)
Ah, ha. Very good.

Duchess
Heavens, my dear Chessel. Do you want me to say it! There's not a more disagreeable man for ten miles around.

Chessel
Bah! Your son-in-law's castle is no more than two miles from here.

Duchess (laughing)
Ah, ah, ah! Very good!

Chessel (going after Félix, who enters.)
Ah, by Jove, Madame. I have to present to you a likeable young man who's just come to my place to recover a bit from the toils of the sea. A future admiral—I'll answer for that. The Vicomte Félix de Vandenesse.

(Félix bows to the Count, Henriette, and the Duchess.)

Count (rising)
Vandenesse? Why, wait a moment, I knew your family well, sir.

Duchess
The Vandenesses, they're one of the oldest families of Touraine.

Félix
Indeed, Duchess.

Count
And, by Jove, I've served in the armies of Louis XVI with a Marquis de Vandenesse.

Félix
My father, sir.

Count (going to Félix)
Your hand, young man, and promise me to come to see us at Château Clocheguarde.

Félix (with joy)
Yes, sir!

Chessel (low)
Château—you'll see, a frightful pigeon cove.

Count
Ah, at my place you won't find the luxury of Mr. Chessel's. I am not a deputy from the Center, Councilor of State and all the rest.

Chessel
Epigrams, my dear neighbor? Feeling better?

Count
Better? Yes, indeed, to the contrary. Here at this moment, my head's like a vise. I have buzzing in my ear, absolutely like the noise of wind in the trees.

(imitating the noise) Whee! Whee! Whee!

Duchess
Annoying!

Count (to Duchess)
Laugh, laugh. Oh, I know, indeed, I pass for a hypochondriac.

Chessel (laughing)
Oh, it's really astonishing how you never complain.

Count
Indeed, I do complain—and with reason—for the way I suffer is unheard of.

Chessel
A vacation will cure you. I am sure that you've almost taken five or six world tours.

(The Count shrugs his shoulders. Chessel bursts out laughing.)

Henriette (to Félix, wanting to change the subject)
But, but, you sir—you've doubtless traveled a lot already?

Félix
Yes, Madame. I spent six years between the sun and the sea.

Chessel
I think so, indeed. At eighteen his tender family sent him to discover America anew.

Félix (low to Chessel)
My friend—

Chessel
And when, three years later, he asked to come rest himself in the paternal foyer, they sent him to find the lost kingdom of Atlantis

Félix
I beg you, sir.

Chessel
Yes, hold on, you're right, I've got to shut up, or rather, let myself go—because I would say too much on the subject of mothers who sacrifice their children—and that would cause pain to the Duchess.

Duchess
What's that mean?

Chessel
Nothing, nothing. I'm going. Félix, will you accompany me? I'm going to take a tour of the rooms.

Félix (hesitating)
But—

Duchess (taking Chessel's arm)
Mr. Chessel, I detest you, but I am never going to leave you.

Chessel
Is that your vengeance?

Duchess
I intend to be sure that you don't speak ill of me to anyone.

Chessel
Speak ill of you, Duchess! Oh! I never repeat what I say to others.

Duchess
You are insupportable.

Félix (bowing to Henriette)
Madame!

Chessel (to the Count)
Au revoir, neighbor.

Count
I bow to you, sir.

Chessel (to Félix)
Are you coming?

(to Count) Goodbye, neighbor!

(Chessel leaves with the Duchess on his arm. Félix follows him, turning to look once more at Henriette.)

Henriette (breathing)
At last.

Count (low to himself)
Neighbor! Neighbor! How insolent that Chessel is with his permanently lucky, his settled handsome face. Neighbor!

Henriette
My friend, if you like, we will leave.

Count
Don't you see all the irony in that "adieu" he threw at me without manners? "Au revoir, neighbor!"

Henriette (sweetly)
It's only a word.

Count
Oh! Why, do you want to know what's in that word?

"Neighbor" means "Here I am, Chessel, Councilor of State, the Deputy from the center, the lucky man. I have a large beautiful estate, an estate which is three times larger and more productive than yours, Mr. Count de Mortsauf." It means, in addition, "As for me, Chessel, I have an immense fortune, and you, Mr. Count, you have a mediocre one. As for me, Chessel, my health is sound and yours is detestable, Monsieur le Comte." All that's not in the dictionary, but that is what "neighbor" means—oof! I can't take it any more.

(The Count collapses in a chair near the chimney.)

Henriette
O my God, what's the matter with you?

Count
Nothing, nothing. A bit tired, need to shut my eyes.

Henriette
I would like to leave. Would you?

Count (almost sleeping)
Leave me alone!

Henriette
He's going to sleep! What to do? I don't dare to insist. Oh, I'd really like to be at home.

(goes to the armchair) Near my daughter, near Madeleine.

(music; Félix returns and stops in the doorway.)

It's time for her to go to bed, poor little thing. Say your prayers for me, tonight, dear angel! If I left you, it's not my fault, do you clearly understand? You don't have to be angry with me about it and if I am not there to close the curtains, at least I am thinking of you. Here, I can pray for you.

Félix (still in the doorway, low)
Oh, how my heart beats!

Henriette (leaning on the back of the arm chair.) My God, spare my dear Madeleine sorrows and tears. Let me take her share of suffering down here. My God! Revoke the civil judgment passed by men. My God, leave me my child.

(her voice expires in suppressed tears)

Félix (aside)
How graceful, how charming.

Henriette (smiling through her tears)
I see you, I see you, Madeleine, your eyes are closing, you are going to see God, as you say sometimes when going to sleep. Goodnight, my little daughter, my child, a last kiss on your pale face, on your discolored lips.

Félix (slowing approaching Henriette)
O my sailor's dreams under the stormy night skies! What were you, tell me, compared to the reality of these enchanting graces—to this sweet reverie full of mystery and love? Sublime storms, waves leaping from the sea in fury—what were you compared to this heart oppressed by a regret or a hope? Oh, why am I not this harmony which caresses you and intoxicates me! Why am I not the flower which places itself on your lips? Why am I not the child who lies on your heart?

(Félix is drawn, as if in spite of himself, he leans over the shoulders of Henriette and his lips graze them. Henriette rises abruptly, uttering a cry.)

Henriette
Sir! Sir!

(Henriette goes to the left.)

Félix (controlling himself)
Oh, my God! Madame! Madame, pardon!

(The Count is still asleep. Arabella returns.)

Arabella (aside)
Ah, bah! Already? Well, I suspected it.

Henriette
Count, Count, wake up.

Arabella (aside)
And the husband is sleeping—charming!

Count (waking with a start)
Huh! What? What's wrong?

Henriette (very agitated)
Let's leave. I beg you.

Count (rising)
You wake me for that? It's unheard of. Do you want to kill me?

Henriette
Mercy, let's go. I feel ill.

Count
By Jove, me, too. I don't feel well, and yet, I'm staying. One owes it to the company. Ah well, since you insist.

(noticing Félix) Ah, it's you, my young friend. Well, I won't say goodbye to you, but until we meet again.

Henriette
Sir!

(stops herself)

Count
Well? Don't you want Mr. de Vandenesse to pay us a visit?

(to Félix) Don't pay any attention. Everyone in Touraine is crazy.

(going to Arabella) Right, milady?

Arabella
My dear sir, I begin to believe so.

(Félix has approached Henriette.)

Félix (to Henriette, low)
My dear lady, pardon me.

(Henriette moves away without replying.)

Count (to Henriette)
Well? Don't you want to leave now? Do you want to go back to the dance?

Henriette (returning)
No, no, my friend.

Count
Then, let's go.

(Chessel enters with Emmeline. Rouvières and Cerny come in from the opposite direction.)

Rouvières (to the Count)
What? You, too? Ah, indeed, the whole world is abandoning me. Here's Mr. Cerny who absolutely wants to retire.

Cerny (meaningfully, looking at Arabella)
Yes, my dear Rouvières, it's necessary that I leave immediately.

Arabella (going to Félix, low)
Ah, Mr. Vandenesse, what torments you are preparing for yourself.

Félix (low)
I don't understand you, Madame.

Arabella
You will waste your time and lose your heart. She won't even grant you a flower.

(aside, playing with her bouquet) And here's a poor bouquet that you disdained? So much the better, it's more original, but I don't want it any more.

(she lets it fall in an arm chair.)

Cerny (aside)
She's tossing me her bouquet. I won't touch it.

(Cerny looks in the mirror.)

Rouvières
Come, since there's no way to retain you.

Chessel (to Count)
Stay, then, Count. They're talking of a supper where everyone will eat. That has to be seen.

(Chessel and the Count continue chatting.)

Félix (to Henriette, while the Count is busy with Chessel)
Madame, in the name of heaven, pardon!

(Henriette abruptly takes her husband's arm as he continues to talk with Chessel. Music. Rouvières goes to Cerny and they chat.)

Emmeline
Ah, now there's a ravishing waltz. Let's go!

Félix
Excuse me, I can't.

Emmeline (vexed)
You refuse me? That's fine! Just you invite me again.

Arabella (who has noticed Félix and Emmeline)
Ah!

Cerny (leaving Rouvières and inviting Emmeline to dance)
Miss?

Emmeline
Certainly, sir, certainly.

(Emmeline goes to the mirror where she examines herself. The Count gives his arm to Henriette.)

Count (ready to leave)
Till soon! Mr. de Vandenesse.

(The Count chats briefly with Félix in the doorway.)

Chessel (aside)
Heavens! The shepherd is inviting the wolf.

Arabella (aside)
Mr. Vandenesse has insulted all three of us, the Countess, Emmeline, and me. It remains to be seen which of us will die of our wounds.

(Arabella bursts out laughing as everyone gets ready to leave.)

CURTAIN

ACT II

The park of the Château Clocheguarde. To the right, a path to the Château. In the foreground, a stone bench. In the back, a hedgerow at a slant. Above it, wheat. To the left, clumps of trees.

At rise, peasants are visible behind the hedgerow, working, coming and going. The Count is near the hedgerow talking to the workers.

Count
Come on, courage, children. The day will be hot, but when you finish your work you will come to the Château and the Countess will pour you a little cup of wine.

Chessel (appearing behind the hedgerow)
Greetings to the residents of Touraine.

Count
Hello! Hello! And your Emmeline? Isn't she with you?

Chessel
Yes, she's coming with her friend Félix.

Count
Mr. de Vandenesse?

Chessel
A morning call, no ceremony. You will allow it? This doesn't damage etiquette too much, huh?

Count
What do you think!

Emmeline (to Félix, who appears behind the hedgerow)
Why come on, Félix, come on! Count, I present to you, Mr. Félix de Vandenesse who this morning horribly tortured my father and me, so that we would bring him here—and now he doesn't dare come forward.

Félix (bowing to the Count)
The fear that a visit so early in the morning—

Count (going to Félix)
In the country! Ah, I warn you, sir, you won't receive Mr. Chessel's gilding and luxury.

Chessel
Fine! Yet another stone in my garden. I will end by having wherewith to build a second Château. That will enrage you, and it will be your fault.

Count (to Félix)
You are looking at a gentleman farmer.

Chessel (to Count)
Tell me, dear neighbor, it seems to me your wheat is much better looking than mine?

Count
Is that yet another jest?

Chessel
No, it's very serious.

Count
Anyway, I give myself a lot of trouble over it!

Chessel
Come on, come on, show me everything.

Count
Willingly. I will rejoin my little Madeleine who I sent to get a little good air. Her mother has a mania for always keeping her shut up.

(to Manette, who enters from the left and goes toward the Château) Manette!

Manette
Sir?

Count
Tell Madame that Miss Emmeline and Mr. Vandenesse are here.

Manette
Yes, sir.

(Manette goes into the castle.)

Count (to Félix)
You see, I am acting without ceremony to put you at your ease. We are going to run over the estate, follow us if you wish, or remain if such is your desire and the Countess will be happy to keep you company.

Chessel (to Count)
Well, I am waiting for you.

Count
Coming! Coming!

Emmeline
Goodbye, my little father.

Chessel (hugging her)
Be good!

Emmeline
Don't be naughty!

Count (laughing)
Ah, oh, good reply!

Chessel (to Count)
Let's wager, Count, that I will walk an hour with you without launching a single epigram?

Count
And are you going to talk?

Chessel
I'm a politician, Count.

Count
It's true!

(pulling out his watch) It's eleven o'clock.

Chessel (pulling out his watch)
At twelve o one, I will tell you my first wicked remark.

(Chessel and the Count disappear to the left.)

Félix (aside)
At last, I am in her home!

Emmeline (following Félix)
Ah, indeed! Félix, I hope you are going to tell me what's been wrong with you—since the ball—since yesterday evening you've not been the same, you no longer talk, you are sulky, you utter sighs enough to turn all the windmills on the plain. I warn you if this continues, I am going to tell my father that I accept my aunt's invitation to go spend two weeks with her in Normandy.

Félix (excitedly)
Oh, no, my good Emmeline, you will refuse, won't you? See what despair will make of me, I who was making such a great celebration of spending a month—a whole month near you, near your father—

Emmeline
Really true? It would cause you pain?

Félix
Oh! More than I can tell you. Think about it! Thirty days of happiness, of hope.

Emmeline
Thirty-one, even. The month of August. Come on, don't be angry. I won't go to my aunt. But, for goodness sake, you will tell me what's the matter with you—what's distressing you?

Félix
I think I was wrong to come here. I am afraid of receiving an ill greeting.

Emmeline
A bad reception from Mr. Mortsauf?

Félix (embarrassed)
No.

Emmeline
From his wife? From Henriette? Why, you are mad. You don't know that Henriette is an angel! You tell me sometimes that I am sweet, that I am good. Well! Imagine on your side, that compared to her, I am a demon, a little monster! So—

Félix
But, if someone had insulted her, offended her?

Emmeline
Insulted, offended, you? Oh, it's not possible—or at least—it was involuntary, it was an error.

Félix (grasping that idea)
Yes, it was an error. But, no matter, it's better to avoid— I'm getting out of here. Goodbye.

(starts to leave)

Emmeline
No time for that, she's here. Don't worry, I will fix all this.

(running to Henriette and hugging her) Hello, my good Henriette.

Henriette (after a frigid greeting to Félix)
Darling little girl, what chance brought you here? Are you leaving us? Are you going to Normandy?

Emmeline (looking at Félix)
My word, no. I don't think so, no. I wanted to have news of you, for you were ill yesterday. You fled like a scared bird. And then, I wanted to bring Félix to you.

(she takes Félix by the hand) Mr. de Vandenesse, my best friend, who persecuted me for four long hours until I brought him here to Clocheguarde. And who, just now, wanted to run off. He was afraid they'd put him out the door.

(Henriette makes no response and takes a step.) Are you going to put on grand airs? Oh, for heavens sake, I can't believe it.

(in a low voice) If he did something to you, he didn't mean to do it.

(laughing) His brain is a little disordered—ever since he got knocked on the head by some savages.

(aloud) Goodbye!

Henriette
Pardon me! I am worried about Madeleine.

Emmeline (stopping her)
Oh! Pretext. You know very well that her father will bring her back.

Henriette
But, Mr. de Vandenesse, who's only here for a short time, would perhaps be very delighted to see the works of the country.

Emmeline
Oh, no! He's horribly tired. Right, Félix?

Félix (embarrassed)
Oh! I—

Emmeline (low)
Make your pardon.

(aloud) Goodbye, I am going to leave you together. You must talk, you must make each other's acquaintance. And once you know each other, I am really sure you will be the best friends in the world. Bye!

(Emmeline runs off. Silence.)

Félix
Yesterday, Madame, I mortally offended you. Permit me to express my deep repentance.

Henriette
Sir, don't remind me of the first—the only outrage—I've ever received in my life.

Félix
I cannot remain under the blows of your rage. I need to excuse myself, to defend myself.

Henriette
Your excuses—your presence here—are an offense.

Félix
Hear me, Madame, for I have to recover my self respect—in your eyes—in mine—and for that it's more than a pardon that I need, it's your goodwill, it's your friendship that I implore.

(Henriette starts)

I am worthy of it, Madame. The affection which Emmeline has for me—this honest, direct and pure heart—must be my guarantee of honesty.

Henriette
Doubtless, but—

Félix
I swear to you, Madame, I am neither insolent nor bold—but a poor sailor who knows nothing of society, nothing of life. It's been so long that I've lived between heaven and the sea, with the storm for a confidant—rude sailors for family—and the bridge of a ship for a country—and that I've lived wandering over unknown fields of an immense sea. I've had only dreams to cast as fodder to my loving impassioned soul.

Henriette
What?

Félix
If you knew the tortures of certain childish souls, poor plants found only on the hard stones of domestic soil.

Henriette
Those tortures. Oh! I know them!

Félix
My mother—why must I accuse her!—my mother repressed my first joys, my first smiles, by the devouring fire of a severe look. I was always sacrificed to my older brother who was the king of the house. He had a preceptor. As for me, I was sent to college each year. I brought back all the most envied awards and when I went to accept them

amidst acclamations and fanfares, I had no one—no one—to embrace me.

Henriette (aside)
The same childhood!

Félix
That's how my youth was spent. Deprived of all joy, of all pleasure. I had a loving heart and nothing to love, but finally, one day, a lucky day for me, a man extended his hand to me. It was Mr. Chessel. Oh, without him, without the affection I had for his child, his little Emmeline, oh, I swear to you, I would be dead of shame.

Henriette
You really must have suffered?

Félix
My classes ended. Without consulting my wishes, a decree of my family sent me to continue my exile at the Naval Academy of Brest. At the end of a year I left as a midshipman. So you can understand, Madame, the delirium which seized me in the ball at the sight of a woman who realized in herself all the beauties, all the dreamed-of graces, of a heart deprived of all joy, deprived of all love.

Henriette (severely)
Sir!

Félix
Oh! Madame, you ought to understand me and absolve me, for you—I've figured it out—you, too, have suffered, and you are still suffering.

Henriette (troubled)
Me, sir? Why no, you are mistaken. I don't know what

you mean.

Félix (abashed)
Pardon, I thought—

Henriette
Can a mother whose child is growing up under her eyes have any greater happiness on earth? Undeceive yourself, sir. I am happy—really happy.

Count (out of sight)
Uncouth peasant!

Henriette
What's wrong?

Félix
Mr. Mortsauf is having a discussion with a worker.

Henriette
O, my God.

(to Count, who appears) My friend, what's the matter?

Count
A worker—who is insulting me in my own home—in front of his own kind—calling me an old fool. My day is spoiled, ruined. I was feeling wondrously well. I was astonished by it myself. My pulse was good, all the alarming symptoms had disappeared. It took this scoundrel—I'm still all upset.

(extending his arm to Henriette) Here, see, Henriette, I'm sure my pulse is over a hundred.

(taking Félix's hand) Feel, feel how my heart is beating. I

will have a crisis. My palpitations. Folks like that will kill me!

Henriette
They are getting too bad. You are so good to them.

Count
Too good! Yes, too good. And you, especially, are too good, too weak. They know that when I kick them out, you will help them in secret and do all that you can for them.

Henriette
It's true. I've been wrong.

Count
By Jove!

(turning and seeming to address the worker who insulted him) Wretch!

Henriette (pulling him back)
Later, my friend. Mr. de Vandenesse is admiring our Clocheguarde.

Count (calming down)
Ah!

(returning to his idea) Scoundrel!

Félix
Indeed, it's a delightful retreat.

Count (appeased)
This is the fruit of revolutions!

Henriette
When the sun has gone down a bit you ought to show your farming to the Vicomte.

Félix
That would be a great pleasure to me, for I am ignorant about that sort of thing.

Count
He's going to try to do that work at the home of Mr. Chessel—

Henriette
My friend!

Count
Yes, you are right. I am doing ill. I don't want to think about that any more. Let's see, what were we talking about? My lands? Well, yes, yes, I will take you over them. We will make a complete course in agriculture.

Henriette
And you, sir, will have an excellent professor.

Count
Why, tonight! He must come, too. We will have a party of whist. You play it?

Félix
It's my favorite game.

Count
Very well. Ah, indeed, the Château, you didn't say anything about it?

Félix
Just now, in passing, I was admiring the facade, a style—

Count
Ah, damn! That must seem very plain to you, really outre in comparison to the sumptuous dwelling of your host—

Félix
Each has its good points. The rich estate of Mr. Chessel is a massive silver plate. Yours, Count, is a jewel case of precious stones.

Count (laughing)
Ah! Ah! If he could hear you, he would be furious. Ah! Ah! A massive silver plate—that's really good, isn't it, Henriette? Ah! Ah! A jewel box of precious stones—that's very well put. See, see, the effect of laughing and of satisfaction. I am must better than before.

Henriette
You see plainly my friend, you ought never to get into a rage.

Count
What—what do you mean? If I get in a rage it's not to amuse myself. Doubtless, I've got my reasons for it. Was I wrong just now?

(Henriette shrugs)

Ah! My God! Don't shrug your shoulders—tell me frankly if I make you pity me for not having common sense—in my own home—before a stranger, like the worker whose side you take—

Henriette
But, my friend, I didn't say anything.

Count
What are you doing here, instead of being near your child who I just saw return to the house quite ill?

Henriette
Madeleine! I didn't know.

Count
Doubtless, you'll send her to take a walk when the sun is hot.

Henriette
Why, no, my friend. It was you who wanted—

Count
Right! It's I who am wrong. Oh, women always want to be right. But, go on, Madame, go after your daughter and put her to bed. For God's sake, when one has children so sick one must know how to care for them.

Henriette
My God! May it be nothing serious!

(Henriette goes back into the Château.)

Count (sitting down)
All this will kill me! All this will kill me!

Félix (aside, looking toward the Château)
Poor victim!

(aloud) I am going to withdraw, sir. I understand that my presence—

Count

No, my friend, no, stay. I am really easy to have someone here who understands me—someone who has common sense. Oh, you see, Mr. de Vandenesse, to live this way, in perpetual anxiety, is intolerable. How do they expect me to recover my health? That is to say, the way I'm going, I don't have six months to live.

Félix

Sir!

Count

Oh, I know whereof I speak. I know my illness. I study it constantly. I've become a doctor and I've prescribed a regimen for myself—reclusive—milk—white fruits—no emotions. In the end, the life of a retiree. You see, my friend, it's not that way here.

Félix

Doubtless, doubtless!

Count

And cares, cares every minute. But, bah! My wife doesn't understand a thing. She doesn't understand how to care for her husband any more than her child. Ah! My God, I don't wish her ill for it. It's not her fault. They never taught— She can't give cares that she never received from her mother. For, my dear sir, Henriette had the most unhappy childhood!

Félix

Yes, right?

Count

My mother-in-law is an egoist. Oh, egoism, I pardon all vices except that. Aren't you of my opinion?

Félix
Yes, Count.

Count
The Duchess never understood her daughter. I recall that when I was paying court to Henriette, and that I read on her face all her inexpressible sadness. I was comparing her to a flower crushed by the gears of a machine of polished steel. That machine was my mother-in- law.

Félix (aside)
Poor woman!

Count
Ah, it was time that I got her out of her hands to give her all the happiness she deserves.

(Félix looks at him in astonishment)

For my poor wife, she's an angel!

Félix
Yes! An angel!

Count
It's all the same, my dear fellow, you're not married. This close contact all your life, this eternal duo of amour obligation—it's something overwhelmingly boring, believe me. Remain a bachelor, it's more relaxing.

Félix (with a guilty emotion)
Pardon, sir, but I believe it's time for me to retire, and—

Count
Come on, you've only been here five minutes. You don't know you must stay to dinner with us. We will make sev-

eral groups of whist and I will have a malicious pleasure in carrying you off from your friend Chessel.

Félix
This is really too kind.

Cerny (entering and speaking to someone off stage.)
Yes, that's it, walk quite slowly, but don't pull too hard on the bridle. Easy! Easy!

Count
Mr. Cerny!

Cerny
Ah, Count.

(bowing to Félix) Sir!

Count
Ah, indeed. You've run the post! It seems to me your horse is white with foam.

Cerny
Yes, yes, it's true, poor beast.

Count
You've got the devil in your pants?

Cerny
My word, almost. But a rose-colored devil, a lively Amazon whose visit I announce to you for certain—your new neighbor.

Count
Ah, bah! Lady Arabella Dudley?

Félix (aside)
She's here—(he moves off)

Cerny
Indeed, I was coming, guilty, to see you, when detouring through a little woods by Aulnay, you know? I noticed Lady Arabella rushing hell for leather in a cloud of dust. I understand—I galloped off—and here I am like an omen.

Count
Ah, indeed, but I don't understand. Lady Arabella—I thought—you're avoiding her now?

Cerny
Always! You know my system—that I developed from you.

Count
It's true.

(to Félix) My dear Mr. Vandenesse, I commend you to Mr. de Cerny—the most ardent fellow in the theory of love. If you need lessons, advice—

Cerny
Laugh! Laugh! She's there—this time, I've got her.

(Arabella enters and gives her arm to Chessel.)

Arabella
Bah! Really, Mr. Vandenesse is here?

Cerny (to Count)
What was I saying?

Count (going to Arabella)
Milady!

Arabella
My God, Count, you are going to think my first visit really strange indeed. But if I displease you, you've only to tell me, and I won't make you suffer my person for a long while. As a new resident, I wanted to pay my respects to the oldest inhabitants of the county. One sees each other once—one judges—and, if you agree, it's marvelous—if the atoms don't match, all is said—this doesn't go any further and one doesn't bow when one meets. Won't I have the pleasure of seeing the Countess?

Count
Yes, truly, milady. She's with her daughter who is a little indisposed.

Arabella
Oh, poor dear child.

Count
But, they must have informed her of your arrival and she's going to come down, I hope—

Arabella
Imagine, I just ran the most charming course. The most comical. I had in front of me the most grotesquely mounted horseman in the world, a grandson of Don Quixote on a descendant of Rosinante.

(laughs)

Count
Ah! Bah!

Cerny (to Count)
She's furious with me!

Arabella
I spied him in a spot in the little woods at Aulnay, and his appearance in the distance appeared so comic, so impossible, that I wanted to give myself the joy of looking him over at my leisure. I launched my horse forthwith, my unknown set off at a gallop so picturesque, so fantastic, that a mad laugh seized me and forced me to slow down the pace. He was jerky, the stirrups beat the flanks of the poor horse, two long thin and ugly legs floated in the wind, a hand clinging to the mane of his mount, another kept pulling on a hat always ready to lose its center of gravity.

(Everyone laughs except Cerny)

Oh, I would have followed him for a week, but I lost sight of him at the turn of a lane approaching here. You don't know him, perhaps?

Chessel
No, no! If my friend de Cerny wasn't here, I would say that perhaps it was he.

Count
Very well—

Cerny (to Chessel)
Sir!

Arabella
What! Ah, bah! It was you? Ah, my dear, you are too good to be true.

Cerny
Milady, I am very lucky.

(low to Chessel) She has tears in her eyes.

Chessel
Yes, from laughing!

(Henriette comes from the Château.)

Count
Well, Madame?

Henriette
Madeleine is better, much better. It won't amount to any-thing.

Arabella (low to Chessel)
There, what was I telling you?

Chessel (low to Arabella)
Bah! You think that Félix—

Arabella (low to Chessel, watching Félix speak to Henri-ette)
I am sure of it.

(curtsying to Henriette) Countess.

Henriette (curtsying)
Milady.

Arabella
You will pardon me, Madame, I hope this visit (casting a glance at Félix) is not inopportune. Perhaps—

Henriette (coldly)
Madame—

Count (offering Arabella a seat)
Milady.

Arabella
Thank you, Count.

Chessel
My word, that's an idea.

(takes a seat) I don't understand a thing. I haven't yet walked on your lands and I'm tired already.

(correcting himself) Ai! That's an epigram.

Count (pulling out his watch)
And it's not yet noon. You lost!

Arabella (low to Chessel, watching Félix)
He doesn't take his eyes off her.

(aloud) Well, Mr. de Vandenesse, are you more gay at noon than at midnight? You were really somber yesterday evening! But you must come see me, in the country, and in Paris especially.

(to Henriette) You'll allow me to steal your friends, Madame?

(Henriette nods, smiling.)

Cerny (aside)
Let's have fun.

Arabella (to Félix)
We will try to distract you. Mr. Cerny will be one of us, he will amuse you.

Cerny
You are too good, milady.

Arabella
No, truly. They say you are a fun guest, that you have a ready wit.

Chessel (laughing)
And he doesn't charge for it.

(Arabella and the Count laugh loudly.)

Cerny (who hasn't understood)
Huh? Excuse me! I didn't hear. I was thinking of something else.

Arabella
Ah! You are charming.

(to Félix) Well, sir, do you accept my invitation?

Félix
Pardon me, Madame, but—

Arabella
Ah, indeed! Why, you detest me, decidedly.

Félix
Not the least bit, Madame.

Arabella
Yes! Yes! I clearly see it. Ah! Take care, I advise people

who detest me, I warn you.

Cerny (aside)
I know it.

Arabella
Yes, that changes me. Stay this way all the time—very cold—very disdainful—and I'll find you adorable.

(to Henriette) Isn't it true, Madame, that it becomes him very well?

Count
Marvelously!

Arabella (to Félix)
But, especially don't take up madrigals—bouquets either. I'll take an aversion to you.

Count (low to Cerny)
She is charming!

Cerny (aside)
Ah! Yes.

Arabella
As for me, I've made my salon a sort of club, a center, a foyer that shines and attracts—where one comes to rekindle one's wit in the fire of conversation. The fire goes out sometimes, but politics relights it, for that's permitted and boredom forbidden.

(to Henriette) You will come there, won't you, Madame, and you'll drag along the Count de Mortsauf.

(to the Count) We will talk politics, Count. I warn you, I

am of the opposition. I am a Whig.

Count
Why's that?

Arabella
Lord Dudley is a Tory. But I am Shakespearean above all.

(to Félix) And you, sir?

Chessel
Oh, him! He's a German!

Félix
Yes, Madame, in fact—

Arabella
A fanatic for Goethe, I wager? Thinking like Werther, and secretly adoring some Charlotte? Are you being frank?

(to Henriette) Dear Madame, it's necessary that we cure him of these follies.

(laughing to Félix) Ah, ah, ah. Werther! Charlotte! Honestly, do you think that happened?

Count
Oh, in Germany—

Arabella
But, those little characters—they don't think, they don't work, they don't love. Especially their love is not love, it's something with a ground glass stopper like ether. Werther spouting phrases and Charlotte rigmarole—pretty story. Come on, true love is another sort of thing, sir. It doesn't amuse itself by putting on a fine dress and pointed hat to

make a sermon over the centuries—it casts gold to the postilions and that's all.

Count
Ah, ah, ah! So you, milady, instead of Werther would have carried off Charlotte?

Arabella
Exactly.

Henriette
But Charlotte had children?

Arabella (vivaciously)
Why didn't she rock them to sleep with her love?

(Henriette looks at her astonished, Arabella rises and changes her tone)

Ah, ah, ah, that's delicious. Now we are quarreling over these imaginary beings. Goethe would really laugh if he heard us. It's all the same, Mr. Vandenesse, believe me. Always choose Marguerite over Charlotte, the Cordelias and the Juliets.

(to Henriette) Madame, I ask you not to disturb yourself. Return to your dear child, the Count will escort me out.

Count
Here's my arm.

Cerny (low to Chessel)
Do you advise me to declare myself?

Chessel (low)
It's now or never.

Arabella (meaningfully)
Till later, Mr. Vandenesse, till later, in Paris.

Félix (bowing)
Madame!

Arabella (after curtseying to Henriette)
Come then, Mr. Chessel—

Cerny
If milady would really allow me, I will go with her?

Arabella
Why, indeed, that would rejoice my heart.

Cerny (to Chessel)
Decidedly I'm going to declare myself.

Chessel
Very nice. It will be funny on horseback.

(Arabella leaves on the Count's arm after a curtsey to Henriette. Chessel follows her with Cerny.)

Félix (watching Lady Arabella)
Oh, you're wasting your time, Lady Arabella.

(pointing to Henriette) Here's the angel. You are the demon, you're wasting your time. It's the angel who will be the object of my life, the reason of my destiny.

Arabella (out of sight)
Stay, I beg you. Goodbye! Goodbye!

(Henriette returns and comes toward the pavilion.)

Félix
Madame, you're going back in already?

Henriette
I am going to see if Madeleine is resting.

(she half opens the door)

Félix
Well—

Henriette (looking)
She's sleeping.

Félix
No need to wake her.

(Henriette comes back)

What's wrong?

Henriette
Why, nothing.

Félix
Oh, yes, I caught a light of joy in your eyes.

Henriette
You could see it?

Félix
Ah, I'm not mistaken.

Henriette
No, at this moment I am happy.

Félix
Truly?

Henriette (in a deep voice)
I was really frightened this morning. I didn't want to frighten my husband and I didn't say anything, but when I learned of Madeleine's sudden indisposition—

Félix
Well?

Henriette
I trembled. For it seems that a terrible children's illness was causing great ravages in Touraine.

Félix (with horror)
Oh!

Henriette
But Madeleine is calm and it was nothing, and I tell you, in truth, I am really happy.

(excitedly) Don't mention it to anyone.

Félix
Oh, don't worry. I have egoism of the heart. I am proud to possess one of your secrets and I don't want to share it with anybody. Oh, thanks—thanks, Madame, for this confidence. It's almost a pardon.

(taking the hand Henriette offers him) You accept me for your friend, right?

Henriette
Doubtless! Aren't you the friend of my husband?

Félix (dully)
Oh, pardon, I am going to offend you, perhaps, but it would be impossible for me to like someone who makes you suffer so much.

Henriette
Sir!

Félix
This morning you told me: "I am happy." And the Count has proven to me that you are telling a sublime lie.

Henriette
Mr. de Vandenesse, I beg you, let's not talk about it any more. I've forgotten yesterday. You forget today.

Félix
I could never.

(Henriette starts to leave, he stops her) A word, Madame, a word more. Are you of the opinion of Lady Arabella who denies holy friendships and mute adorations?

Henriette
Why do you ask me that?

Félix
Because, if it was that way—I'd be the most wretched of men, for I've sworn to devote my life to you.

Henriette
Ah, be quiet, sir.

Félix
Don't reject humble friendship which asks to make itself your support. Friendship, only friendship. In the name of

heaven, Madame, don't prevent me from believing in it.

Henriette
Sir, I don't understand. Who gave you the right to speak to me like this?

Félix
Your sufferings, Madame. The forlorn condition in which you live. The injustices of those you love.

Henriette
Sir, it's not for you to judge the actions of the Count. Besides, you are unjust to him. This morning he was nervous, irritable and ill, but he is rarely so. And I repeat to you, he loves me and I am happy.

Félix
Pardon! Pardon! But I don't believe you.

Henriette
Sir—

Félix
Oh, now, you see, Madame, you can really scorn me, hate me, kick me out even, but you cannot hide from me either your sufferings or your tears, for I've understood everything. I've read only one page of your life, and I've understood it in its entirety. I know we've had the same mother—adversity. Accept my devotion, adopt my heart, that poor orphan has nothing to love, and I swear to you there's no place in that heart except for respect and self-sacrifice. My lips will open only to pity or console you. My only desire will be to make you happy. My only joy will be to make you smile. I will never dream of others, I swear to you on what I hold most dear, I swear to you on the life of Madeleine.

Henriette (with a scream)
Ah! what have you said? You've frightened me! Retract that oath. I don't accept it.

Félix
You doubt me then, Madame?

Henriette
Don't question me! You are driving me crazy. It seems I'm dreaming.

Emmeline (entering)
They're still at it? Peace hasn't been made?

Henriette
My God! My God! Is it true one could be loved like this?

Félix (to Henriette)
You are weeping, you've wept in front of me! You accept me then for a friend. Oh, counting from today your tears will never flow more silently. I will be here to gather them, to dry them.

Emmeline (mechanically plaiting a crown of sunflowers)
What's he saying?

Félix
Oh, how beautiful life seems to me! How the days are going to seem short. I am going to have the right to read in your eyes, in your soul, and Madame, your darling child, how I am going to love her. There will be two of us to watch over her. With us nearby, misfortune cannot reach her.

Henriette (aside)
O my God! Forgive me for the happiness I feel in listening

to him.

Félix (wanting to take Henriette's hand)
Your hand, my friend, my sister!

Emmeline (aside)
My God! What's wrong with me? Am I jealous?

Félix
You don't answer me, but your hand is trembling. You are smiling at me. Oh, you believe in me! Thanks! Thanks!

(Félix kisses Henriette's hand deliriously. Henriette, troubled, withdraws it. Emmeline, with a stifled scream, drops her flowers.)

Emmeline
Oh, I understand everything. I love him!

Henriette (noticing her)
Emmeline—

Félix
Her!

(Emmeline quickly stealthily dries her tears.)

Henriette
Come on!

Emmeline
Here I am.

(Emmeline wants to walk, but staggers and is sustained by Félix.)

Félix
Emmeline, my child, what's the matter with you?

Emmeline (smiling)
Nothing, nothing. I was running. I jostled my foot against a stone. I felt ill and let my flowers fall.

Henriette
How pale she is!

Emmeline
Pale? Me? Oh, for goodness sake, my head is burning. Well, are you reconciled?

Félix
Yes, yes, thanks to you, Emmeline.

Emmeline
Yes, thanks to me! And I am really happy about it.

(holding back tears) Really happy!

Chessel (coming in with the Count)
Ah, there you are, Emmeline. I was looking for you. I want to return. You know I have to write to your aunt.

Emmeline
Yes, yes! It's true. Let's leave. Come, Félix, goodbye, Henriette.

Count
One moment! One moment! The devil! What a rush Miss Emmeline is in to leave us, but I won't hear of it. First of all, you are all dining here—

Emmeline
Sir, but my father has to write—

Count
He will write in my office. And now, a serious question.

Chessel (laughing)
Let's see?

Count
Are you decidedly going to Normandy?

Chessel
Why, I—

(Chessel looks at Emmeline.)

Emmeline
Yes, yes, sir. We are leaving tomorrow.

Chessel
Feather-brain, go. This morning she wouldn't hear talk of this voyage.

Félix (low)
Indeed, you promised me?

Emmeline
Yes, but I reconsidered. We have to. My aunt would be furious! And then, it's very amusing at her place. You dance every day, play at proverbs, she's charming, and—

(lowering her eyes) You have to come with us.

Count
Pardon! Pardon! Now, that's exactly where I'd like to

come in. Mr. de Vandenesse is no longer your guest. He's become mine.

Emmeline (aside)
Ah, my God!

Count
I am inheriting our dear sailor. I would have preferred to steal him from you, but alas!

Chessel
My word, my dear Count, you will have done something good in your life. For this poor Félix has traveled enough and doesn't need to see Normandy, and on the other side, he'd die of boredom alone in our hermitage.

Count
It's agreed then.

(to Félix) You accept? (Félix nods affirmatively)

Bravo!

Emmeline (aside, sadly)
He's staying.

(The bell of the Château can be heard.)

Chessel
There's the dinner bell.

Count (to Félix)
Félix, offer your arm to my wife.

(Félix gives his arm to Henriette. The Count offers his to Emmeline.)

Emmeline
Pardon, sir, I'll follow you. I forgot my flowers.

(Henriette and Félix have already disappeared. Emmeline picks up her flowers and when she finds herself alone, she collapses on a bench.)

Emmeline (weeping)
Oh, mother! Mother!

CURTAIN

ACT III

A room with a door at the back giving on the porch. A large window on each side of the door. To the left a chimney with a clock and flowers. In front of the chimney a table for whist. Doors left and right. A sofa, a round table around which are seated: to the left the Count, facing the audience Félix, to the right Henriette. Chessel is seated at the whist table reading a paper. Félix is sketching. Henriette is embroidering. The Count is reading an old book.

Count
Sometimes in these old medical books there are observations full of justice. Yes, that's really so. It's my illness. I couldn't describe it better. The diagnosis is exact and the phenomenal symptoms are indeed the same. We shall see about the treatment.

(flips through the book)

Henriette (watching what Félix is doing)
Is it still my portrait you are doing?

Félix
A rough draft.

Henriette
That album is full. You know me by heart.

Count

Well, now I'm convinced of it, my dear Félix. The regimen I've imposed on myself for so long is worthless. I've made admirable discoveries in this book.

Félix (as he sketches)
Really.

Chessel

Count, have you discovered that the heart is on the right?

Count (sharply)
For those who don't have one, it's neither right nor left, sir.

Félix (laughing)
To Mr. Chessel, postage paid.

Count

My word. He's something unheard of, this Chessel. Gone two weeks with his daughter—in Normandy—two weeks the three of us spent in paradise. Right, Henriette? Here he is back again. He runs immediately on arriving to pay me his first visit. You might think it was from friendship. Ah, indeed, yes! It's to renew his war of pin pricks.

Chessel

It's still true, but it's not my fault if we came this evening. It's my daughter. It's Emmeline who wished it. I confess I would have waited until tomorrow to see you, but she couldn't do without you. That is to say, that two hours after we returned: "Father, let's go say good evening to Henriette. Father, let's go get news of the Count and Madeleine!" That was her refrain.

Henriette
She loves us a lot. We return it. But, it's cold tonight, you must tell Emmeline to return, Mr. Chessel.

Chessel (going to the rear and calling)
Emmeline!

Emmeline (in the garden)
I'm here!

Count (rapping with joy on his book)
I'm keeping to the treatment I need. Just the contrary of what I was doing. Dark vegetables, game, good wine, and rest. By Jove, with my monk's life, I was killing myself.

(The Count rises. Emmeline comes in and sits on the sofa at the right.)

Chessel
It's plain!

(looking at Félix's drawing) There, there, there! Why, it's very nice. Decidedly you have a talent of the first order. It's a very good likeness.

Count (looking)
Yes, not bad. But it's flattering.

Chessel
Always loveable, these dear husbands.

Henriette
Always true. That's more valuable.

Count
It's suffocating here.

(opens the window and leans on the balcony; to Chessel who has followed him) It seems to me that Emmeline is a little sad, a little pensive.

Chessel (laughing)
It's her seventeen years singing in her heart and she doesn't understand.

Félix
Come, Emmeline. You are going to make observations for me—critiques.

Emmeline
Me?

Henriette
It's true. You draw.

Emmeline (going to Félix)
I used to draw, but I no longer do so.

Chessel (leaving the window)
She used to sing, and she no longer sings. She used to laugh, and she no longer laughs. She used to talk, and she no longer talks. That's not a bad thing!

(hugging her) Dear child, go, this will pass of.

(aside) With wedding bells.

Count (at the window)
A real summer night. The flowers smell sweet.

Henriette (pulling Emmeline aside)
What's wrong with you, child?

Emmeline (resisting lightly)
Me? Nothing.

Félix
Ah, my good Emmeline, my goddaughter. We are getting angry. You no longer say a word to me. You have great sorrows that you are hiding from me. You are returning from a long trip without jumping on my neck. You don't behave like that with a relative.

(pulling her gently to him) Look, why these tears in those big eyes? Is it because you found your favorite flower withered, broken by the wind? No? The favorite bird of your bird cage flew away, the ingrate? No? I see what it is: the poor people of the valley have exhausted your deep secrets. There still remain some unfortunates to succor?

Emmeline (grasping that idea)
Yes, yes. Exactly. Some unfortunates. There are so many.

Count
Pretenders who joke of dying of hunger.

Chessel (laughing)
The Sardanapaleses!

Félix
My goddaughter refuses to associate me with her good works?

(giving her his purse) Here's for the poor.

(opening a box and placing it next to her) And here's for you. Choose a picture. It's the work of my two week stay at Clocheguarde.

Chessel (by the table)
Ah! It's a view of the castle.

Count (between Chessel and Félix)
It's striking!

Chessel
And it doesn't flatter. Say, Félix, now that we're back, we reclaim you. Right, Emmeline?

(Emmeline doesn't answer.)

Count
Huh?

Chessel
You allow us, Countess?

Henriette (hesitating as Félix watches)
It's a right.

Count
Stop there, if you please. I put in my veto.

Chessel
What?

Emmeline (looking at the picture and repressing tears)
Her portrait—always!

Count
Félix is my guest. You put him out the door very impolitely—and I harbored him. We get along marvelously. He understands me. He listens to me. He's very good at whist.

Chessel
To be beaten—

Count
Consequently, I'm keeping him.

Chessel (laughing)
Gone!

Emmeline (putting her hand to her eyes)
He's staying.

Henriette
Well! What's wrong with you, Emmeline?

Emmeline (troubled)
Me? Nothing!

Chessel
Tears?

Emmeline (embarrassed, leafing through the pictures)
It's nothing. It's this drawing which recalls a memory.

Henriette
What is it?

Félix
You know, Madame, that very picturesque little corner of the cemetery in the valley? Why these sad ideas, Emmeline? Choose another one.

Emmeline (weeping)
No, Félix, no. I'm keeping it. My mother is there.

Félix
Oh, how angry I am.

Chessel
Cursed drawing.

Emmeline (rising)
Father, you must be worn out by our trip. Come, let's retire.

Count
What, already?

Henriette
Why, it's impossible. You are still quite upset.

Emmeline
It's all the same.

Chessel
You want to?

Emmeline
Yes.

Count
Wait at least until I light the lantern, for it's as dark as in an oven.

(The Count lights a lantern which he takes from the chimney.)

Emmeline
Goodbye, goodbye, Félix. Goodbye, Henriette.

Henriette
Well! You aren't going to kiss me?

Emmeline
Pardon!

(kisses her)

Henriette
I will go tomorrow morning to get news about you.

Emmeline
Yes, yes, that's it.

(controlling her tears and forcing herself to smile) Till tomorrow! Till tomorrow!

Chessel (giving his arm to Emmeline)
Goodbye. Stay, we can see perfectly. Our lantern suffices.

(The Count has passed in front of Chessel who follows him with Emmeline. Henriette accompanies them. Félix, holding the lamp, remains on the steps.)

Henriette
Till tomorrow.

Chessel (now out of sight)
Till tomorrow.

(Henriette returns.)

Félix
How happy I am to be alone with you for a moment.

Henriette
Why is that? What have you to say to me?

Félix (tenderly)
A thousand things when I am far from you—and nothing—not a thing when you are here.

Henriette
Félix, you know on what conditions I accepted your friendship and your devotion.

Félix (sighing)
Yes, I condemned myself to silence; but everything speaks in me.

(pointing to the valley through the window to the left) These last white lights which illuminate the valley, this evening breeze which rocks the poplars, these great trees with silver leaves always trembling, these flowers which surround us, all these things have a language, a song full of mysterious and tender notes—and nothing forces them to keep their secret—no law obliges them to be silent.

Henriette (pensively)
It's true—

Félix
See that lily which balances on its fragile stem? Doesn't it represent to you the pure shining loved woman who receives, like incense, all the perfume from the flowers that surround it?

Henriette (a little troubled)
Yes, but see further off that bright rose, surrounded and protected by its hardly opened buds? It's the mother of the family. Look! The different stems of the flowers press

about it in vain. The blindweed is trying to embrace her in its spirals, but the mother of the family remains, and will remain, passive, radiant, and protected by her children until her last leaf falls with her last rosy tear.

Félix (humbly)
Oh, pardon! Pardon!

Henriette (moving away)
Félix, Félix, I beg you. Don't ever talk to me this way. For if it ever happens again—

Félix
Well?

Henriette
I'll have to exile you from my heart.

(sits)

Félix (finishing Henriette's thought)
And from your house? But then, who will help you bear the life you lead? Who will take a share of your domestic sorrows? Who will be—I won't say devoted enough—but patient enough—to bend to the yoke of your husband? Who will amuse him in his motiveless sadness, calm his childish rages and quell his unforeseen furies?

Henriette
Félix, is that a reproach you are making me?

Félix
No, it's a fear which grasps my heart. Oh, I will stay. I will stay. I accept all the conditions you've made. I will impose silence on the wild spirits of my soul. I will put all my joys into my unknown sacrifices, in my tacit immolations. My

joy will be to offer myself willingly to the blows of the despot and when you've pressed my hand, when a caress from your eyes tells me "courage" I will think myself well paid for my trouble.

Henriette (offering him her hand)
Here, you are a child!

(Félix kisses her hand with intoxication) Take care, friendship which demands such a favor is really dangerous.

Count (outside)
Hold the light, Manette. You could break your neck.

Félix
Here's the master.

Henriette
He's going to want to play cards, saying he doesn't care for it, when he's dying to. Do like you did yesterday. That was very good. Seem to force his hand.

Félix
And especially—don't win!

Henriette
That's the difficulty.

Félix
I will try, but luck is sometimes headstrong.

(Henriette smiles. Félix takes his place at the table. Manette come in with a candle. The Count follows.)

Count
They are leaving us in darkness, groping about blindly. It's

unheard of!

(The Count sits at the table.)

Count
Manette, close up.

(yawning) Ah!

(Manette closes the door and the shutters and the curtains then withdraws.)

Henriette (to Count, who prolongs his yawning)
Oh, sir—

Count
Well, what? Sir! Nervous, by Jove, with a friend, and I am going to bother myself. I don't feel well this evening. Ah, indeed. What holiday is it tomorrow that they are making so much fuss about?

(Henriette and Félix exchange a bewildered look.)

Félix
. What?

Count
Well, what? What is it you have to look at? Didn't you hear the bells ringing for the last quarter of an hour?

Henriette (hesitating)
No!

Count
Ah, indeed, you must both be deaf. You didn't hear the chimes from the village?

Félix
Oh, yes, yes. Now I understand perfectly.

Count
To the other one—who hears bells at the moment they no longer ring—wait—now it's starting again.

Henriette
Yes, indeed. I think I hear—

Félix (low to Henriette)
I don't hear anything.

Henriette
Me neither. I'm afraid of some terrible crisis.

Count
It's a sinister noise which I can't bear. Who is dead?

Félix
Would you, Count, play a game of whist with us? The noise of the dice will distract you.

Count (with affected indifference)
Oh, it's too late. And then, it won't amuse you very much. You've lost already.

Henriette
They are excellent lessons.

Count
Oh, I don't pose as a professor, but—practice—

Félix
I don't wish to abuse your good nature, and it's really fine of you to contest with a dunce like me.

Count
Whatever pleases you at the moment. Let's see. Where shall we place ourselves?

Félix
There.

Count (sitting at the table, back to the chimney)
What are we playing for?

Félix (sitting down facing the Count)
Like always, one sou per point.

Count
Bah! Let's play two sous. That will make you pay more attention. You won't need as many lessons.

Félix
I am going to apply myself.

(Félix and the Count toss the dice to see who will begin. They play.)

Count (as he plays)
Henriette?

Henriette
My friend?

Count
Have you received news from your mother?

Henriette
No, and that makes me uneasy. I've written to her several times. I asked her if she would come spend several days with us and she hasn't yet answered me.

Count
Ah, it's incredible! Always these execrable dice.

Henriette (who has risen, low to Félix)
Be careful.

Félix (low, while shaking the dice box)
I am doing all I can.

(tossing the dice)

Count (striking the table)
Right! That's all it needs. And him—he brings whatever he must. Oh, the joy is gone. I'm going. The variations tire my poor head.

Félix (low to Henriette)
I can't change the dice.

Count
And, God be thanks, you are going like a mad bull. Did we say what we were playing for?

Félix
Why, yes. Two sous per pint.

Count
Why two sous? One sou as usual. That's quite enough.

(The Count rises and drinks some sugared water which he finds by the chimney.)

Henriette (low to Félix)
I tremble.

Félix (low)
I've changed the set. He will win.

Count (coming back to sit)
Come on! Come on! Finish beating me, but at least murder me by the rules.

Henriette (leaning over the Count's chair)
Let's see, my friend. I am sure you are going to recover your losses and win.

Count
Whose trick was that?

Félix
It was yours, I believe, Count.

Count (looking at his trick surprised)
Ah, let's see a bit.

(reflecting) I must be losing my head. Whose trick is that?

Félix (a bit embarrassed)
It's—yours.

Count
Why, by Jove! No! No! It's not mine. They changed it. There were four ladies on this row, and I had taken a drubbing.

Henriette
Still, my friend—

Count
Still—still. I know what I say. I have my head, thank God! And yet, once more, this trick is not mine.

Félix
Perhaps we jostled the table.

Count
There's no way of jostling the table to make ladies slip from little fan to join big fan.

(furious) I tell you, sir, you moved my tricks.

Henriette (to Félix, low)
Confess, confess.

Félix (with constraint)
Well, sir. I owe you a sincere admission. I wanted to spare you a defeat which appeared to annoy you greatly, and I took the liberty—

Count (blowing up, rising)
Damnation! Does he take me for a child? For an idiot? Or have the two of you sworn to drive me crazy? Just now, you denied the sound of bells that were ringing in my ears, now you pretend to me the trick that was changed was my trick.

Henriette
Why, my friend, it was with the intent—

Count
It was with one intent—to turn me into ridicule. To make fun of me, to make me pass for a tyrant—to pose as a victim. If there's a victim here, it's me.

Félix (indignant)
You?

Count (brutally)
Was I talking to you? By what right do you raise your voice? You are here—in my home—do you understand? But no, my home is no longer my home. They cheat here. It's a gambling den! Oh, I am suffocating, there's no air here.

(going to the chimney) There are the flowers which cramp my temples and which asphyxiate me! This is where you put them deliberately. They want to kill me! They shan't succeed!

(throws the flowers on the ground and tramples them under his feet) Ah, I cannot take it any more. Some air, some air!

(The Count opens the window at the left.)

Henriette (listening)
Ah, my God! Do you hear? In the courtyard, the noise of a carriage.

Félix
Indeed, some unforeseen visit. I am going to tell—

Manette (running in)
Madame! Madame!

Henriette
What is it?

Manette
Madame, it's a post carriage. And the mother of Madame is getting out. She wanted to come through the garden—

Henriette
My mother!

Félix (to Manette)
That's fine. Before opening, help me. God! What a mess.

(Manette and Félix bring the table from the back to the right, then Manette leaves.)

Henriette (going to the Count)
My friend, my friend, get hold of yourself.

Count
Huh?

Henriette
It's my mother, my mother.

Count (as if he has just awakened)
Well, your mother? So, what about her?

Henriette
She's coming to see us. She's getting out of the carriage.

Count (getting control of himself little by little)
Ah, yes. The Duchess de Lenoncourt! Well! Let her come through the gate of honor. Let torches be lit. Let my servants light up the place!

Henriette (to Félix)
Open, open.

Duchess (entering)
Ah! Why, indeed, this is a fortress. You hear the hinges creak, and the moaning of bolts.

Count (guided by Henriette)
Duchess.

(bowing)

Duchess
Say, this is a stronghold, your house. It's paradise and you only get in by cunning.

(pointing to Félix) And this gentleman, who performs the function of gate keeper—

Henriette
Mother—

Count (giving her an armchair)
Madame, if we'd known the honor which was reserved for us—

Duchess (sitting)
Indeed, you weren't expecting me. I wanted to surprise you.

Henriette
Mother, you couldn't have done so more agreeably.

Duchess
Do you think so? It's that I find you at sixes and sevens. So strange. One would say my coming has upset you.

Count
Could you believe that?

Duchess
It's nothing. So much the better. Let's not talk about it any more.

(to Henriette) Why, you didn't tell me in your letters that Mr. de Vandenesse was installed here with you. I thought he was with Mr. Chessel. All the same, sir, I am charmed to see you here. I have good news to announce to you.

Félix
To me, Madame?

Duchess
To you, sir. But, let's proceed in an orderly way. I've got the good news in my pockets.

(aside) Lady Arabella didn't deceive me.

(aloud) Ah, indeed, you live here like veritable owls. And meanwhile, in Paris, everyone is taking his share of the cake of indemnity. Those who have the naïveté not to put out their hand won't have a blade of straw. I've seen King Louis XVIII. His Majesty was of a perfect grace. He sends you this parchment, the Cross of St. Louis, and he promised me to include you in the first batch of the Peers of France.

Count (with enthusiasm)
Such a favor! Oh, that makes me ten years younger.

Duchess
There's still that, at least.

(The Count moves near Félix.)

Henriette (taking her mother's hand)
Madame, how grateful!

Duchess (to Félix)
For you, sir, here's what I have to announce to you: a let-

ter from your mother recalling you to Paris immediately.

Félix
To Paris?

Duchess
To Paris. Read, read, you're allowed.

(Félix peruses the letter) Madame de Vandenesse, through Lady Arabella's influence has obtained a charming position for you. You are no longer a sailor, you are leaving as an ambassador's secretary—in London.

Count
Why, you are a beautiful fairy, Duchess.

Duchess
The Good News Fairy!

(to Félix) Well, sir! Aren't you jumping with joy? Aren't you transported, ravished?

Henriette
It's doubtless a surprise, an astonishment.

Duchess (rising, severely to her daughter)
Does the gentleman need an interpreter to explain himself?

Félix
Indeed, I was so little prepared for this news—

Duchess
Ah, indeed! But, aren't you ambitious?

Félix (looking at Henriette)
Yes, Madame, I have one ambition—

Duchess
One! That's not enough. You need to have a spare.

Count
Bah! Félix is young. Ambition will come later.

Duchess (aside, looking at the Count with deep disdain)
Husband!

(aloud) After all, what they told me is doubtless true?

Count (with a different feeling)
What's that?

Duchess
The Vicomte, perhaps, never wants to leave the country.

Count
Why is that?

Duchess
The rumor is running that he's retained by some romance, some love affair.

Félix
Madame, I swear to you—

Count
Him? A romance, a love affair? Come on! Since he got here, he hasn't taken a step out of the Château, except to go for a stroll with me or Henriette. Henriette can tell you.

Henriette (embarrassed)
No doubt.

Duchess
No matter. Before making a decision, Vicomte. Read and reread the letter from your excellent mother. Go meditate over it, if it seems good to you. We won't be insulted.

Félix (bowing)
Madame!

Duchess
You, Count, I will be obliged if you would take a look at my people and my carriage.

Count
At your disposal, Duchess. Come, Félix, come. We are going to talk all this over.

(low to Duchess) I'll try to confess him, but between you and me, I'm convinced there's not the least thing.

(The Count takes Félix by the arm and leaves with him.)

Duchess (to herself, watching the Count leave)
Ah, double husbands.

Henriette (to herself)
I am not guilty, she's my mother, and yet, I'm trembling.

Duchess
Do you know, my darling, that my son-in-law has become very amiable?

Henriette
He's an excellent husband, mother.

Duchess
Well, now, that's a great pleasure for me to hear. For, if

you recollect, you didn't want him. I imposed him on you.

Henriette
I'd forgotten that.

Duchess
Ingrate! My word, since we are on the conjugal terrain, let's pursue it. I don't have a lot of time to give you either. I did my sixty miles to surprise and embrace you. I am tired, I need some rest. I frankly broach the question.

Henriette (upset)
What do you mean?

Duchess
Oh, for the love of heaven! Don't play games. Let's be natural, if it's possible. Or rather, let's agree on our parts. I'm going to take my fan and put on rouge. I have just enough.

Henriette
Mother, I assure you—

Duchess
We won't put on rouge? Good. I prefer that.

(taking her hand) Look, dear little girl, since, by your confession, Mr. de Mortsauf is an excellent husband, why cheat on him?

Henriette (forcefully)
Cheat on him! Me? What do you mean?

Duchess
Why, they are saying it all over the Court, in Paris.

Henriette
And what are they saying, mother?

Duchess
They say, my darling, that Mr. de Vandenesse is your lover.

Henriette (hardly able to repeat the word)
My lov—

Duchess
What do you call it in Touraine?

Henriette
Mr. Félix, my lover! Ah, mother, you don't believe it! It's false, I swear to you. My God, what must I say, what must I do to prove to everyone? To prove to you, especially, that it is not true?

Duchess
It's necessary, that tonight, tomorrow at the latest, that Mr. de Vandenesse return to his post. That's all.

Henriette
He will leave. I swear to you.

Duchess
Fine! I didn't expect less from your reason. I thought that, indeed, as a Lenoncourt, my daughter wasn't mad woman enough to want to keep for her profit, the life of a young man for whom the most brilliant future is reserved. I couldn't believe that she'd put to sleep all legitimate ambition in the young man's heart by cradling him in a hope that must always be deceived. A woman like you must realize that this lover, ceaselessly deluded, will come one day to demand an account of his lost youth and of his

completely compromised future.

Henriette (bowing her head)
It's true! It's true!

Duchess
She must think that the appearance of a sin (rising) is the sin itself, and that the ridicule falling on her spouse reflects on the wife and on her child.

Henriette
Madeleine!

Duchess
That's all that I had to tell you. I will stop here, if you like, with my moral instruction, for I am falling asleep. Goodnight.

Henriette (wanting to retain her)
Mother!

Duchess
Oh, desolated, my darling. I am exhausted. My throat is on fire. I cannot talk except to my pillow. Goodbye.

(The Duchess goes out.)

Henriette
Leave, yes, yes. He must leave, for the world doesn't believe in pure friendships, voluntary brotherhoods. Is it so impossible? My God! Oh, yes, yes, I feel it now. I was mad when I thought I could, without crime, pour my sufferings into his heart and my cries of despair—(with big sobs)

Yes, yes, you will leave, dear friend of my heart, and I will remain alone, faithful to your memory, for I love you. I love you!

Count (off)
Goodnight, Félix. Goodnight, my friend.

Henriette
The Count!

Count (entering, to Félix off)
Go on, I will excuse you with my wife, without hard feelings.

(to Henriette) Ah, you're still here, Henriette. I thought you were in your room.

Henriette (a little troubled)
No, no. I was finishing this work.

Count
Well, I've spoken to Félix. He had nothing to do with it, and we've discovered where this came from.

Henriette
Ah—

Count
It's evidently from Lady Arabella, who the other day left furious with Félix because of his coldness and his indifference to her.

Henriette
You think so?

Count
It's astonishing, this evening, I who am always the first to

feel sleepy, I don't have any wish to sleep. Chevalier de Saint Louis. Peer of France! That's superb.

Henriette
My friend, if you permit it, I am going to withdraw. I have some letters to write.

Count (sitting on the couch)
One moment. Come here, Henriette, I have to speak to you.

Henriette (uneasy)
To me?

Count
I have to ask my pardon for what happened this evening.

Henriette
What for?

Count
My rage at backgammon. Come over here.

Henriette (near the table)
I'm straightening out my work.

Count
Then, I will go to you.

Henriette (going to him)
I'm here.

Count (pulling her closer)
Sit, then.

(she sits on a chair by the sofa) How your hand is trembling.

Henriette
You think so?

Count
I've been really bad, haven't I?

Henriette
Oh, well, a gesture of impatience—

Count
No, heavens, really. I behaved badly with poor Félix and with you yourself. I humbly ask your pardon. Will you forgive me?

Henriette (trying to disengage her hand)
Oh, quite willingly.

Count
You tell me that through good nature. You are still angry with me, I am sure of it.

Henriette
Why no, I swear to you, Count.

Count
Nothing except the cold way you say it. Count is fine in society, but when we are alone—(she pulls her hand away)

(tenderly) Look how you are. You take your clever white hands away from me. I love you so much! You are bitter, that's bad.

Henriette
Why, no!

Count

Coquette! I must go down on my knees to implore mercy.

(he kneels to her) Eh, well, look. Me, a man, me with grey hair. Me, the master, I am on my knees to the slave and I await my pardon with a glance.

Henriette

My friend, I must go. I have to write—

Count

You send me away, you, my adored wife, the good genius of my home, you that I've loved from the first day—

Henriette (rising)

Count!

Count

Huh? What? Is it horror that I inspire in you? Now, see my life! Everyone here detests me. Wife! Valets, even Madeleine herself, Madeleine, my child. If I speak to her, she trembles at my voice. If I come close to hug her, I see her turn away to avoid me, like you, Madame.

(going to Henriette) And yet, you are my wife; my wife before God and before men. The mother of a child that's mine. She is really mine, my child?

Henriette

Ah! You are making me ill!

Count (shouting)

You, too. You are making me ill. You are killing me.

Henriette

Lower, lower. They could hear you.

Count
And if I want to speak loud, if I want to scream my indignation?

Henriette
From pity!

Count
Eh! As for you, you are truly without pity for me. Go. You are a monster of hypocrisy.

(The Count pushes Henriette violently. She falls, overwhelmed, into an armchair at the left. Félix runs in from the door at the left.)

Félix
My God, those shouts.

(goes to Henriette)

Count
Ah, it's you. Heavens, Félix. Indeed, you see this woman? She has only scorn and hate for me.

Henriette (in pain, rising)
Sir!

Count
This woman, she is lying to men and to God and, indeed, thinks herself a saint.

Félix
But, you are killing her, sir.

Count
Ah! You are against me, too, are you? She's bewitched

you. Encourage her in her crime, be her accomplice. Kill me, kill your friend.

(The Count leaves. Félix kneels by Henriette and tries to revive her.)

Félix
Henriette! Henriette! Come to. It's me, it's your friend. It's Félix.

Henriette (opening her eyes, in a weak voice)
Félix—

Félix
I've just answered my mother. Don't be afraid. I've refused and I'm staying—near you, always. We will be together.

(Félix raises Henriette and supports her. She clings to him, frightened.)

Henriette
Oh, yes! You'll stay, won't you? Don't leave me! Don't leave me!

Félix
Calm down, lean on me, your brother. Dry your tears.

Henriette (standing, very weak, leaning on Félix)
What happened? How did I get near you in the middle of the night?

(with a cry) Ah, I recollect. My mother, the Count, my oath, everything! And you are still here.

(with terror) Leave! Leave!

Félix
Never!

Henriette
Tomorrow. Tomorrow, you will leave Clocheguarde. You must.

(with feverish volubility) The road to fortune is open to you; go! I will write you often, very often. Wait, this very night I am going set forth a rule of conduct for you to follow all your life.

(with fictitious gaiety) Then, sometimes, you will come here. You will take a rest from the world and tell me your triumphs, your struggles. That's agreed, right? You don't say anything? Why, speak then, speak!

Félix
Henriette, tell me! Your mother spoke to you, right? She demanded that I leave?

Henriette (struggling against her emotion)
No, no. It's I alone—I—Oh, tell me you will leave.

Félix (in despair)
Kicked out, kicked out! Now see the fruit of my mute sufferings and my secret despair.

Henriette
Be quiet! Be quiet!

Félix
It wasn't enough to demand from my ardent youth a brother's friendship, a childish docility, when I felt in my heart the shudders of the most exalted love.

Henriette
From pity!

Félix
Oh, you will know all that I've suffered.

Henriette (exploding)
Do you think that I am unaware of it?

Félix
Henriette, you love me!

Henriette (with a sort of distraction)
Well, yes. Yes, I love you, and it's for that, it's because I see the terrible danger threatening that I tell you to flee. I'm afraid of you, I'm afraid of me.

(begging) Leave! Leave!

Félix (with tears)
Oh, don't say that word; it kills me.

Henriette
Oh, don't weep, for I need all my courage, and I feel myself weakening. It's abandoning me. Mercy! Hide your tears from me.

Félix
Henriette—

Henriette
Oh, my mind is wondering. My reason is lost. I have no consciousness of anything. Leave me, go away!

Félix
Henriette, I love you!

Manette (running in)
Madame! Madame, I don't know what's wrong with Madeleine!

Henriette
My child, I was forgetting you.

(to Félix) You will leave, sir, you will leave.

(Henriette rushes out of the room.)

CURTAIN

ACT IV

Arabella's. A boudoir opening on rooms prepared for a party. A dressing table to the right.

Duchess (standing over Arabella, adjusting her hair)
One more flower here and you will be ravishing. There. Really, that gives you a bit of a pastoral air that becomes you nicely.

Arabella
Ah, Duchess, you are wasting your time putting all of Spring in my hair. You won't make me smile any more for that.

Duchess (sitting beside her)
By the way, why did you make me come two hours before everyone else?

Arabella
We have to talk.

Duchess
Really! What's it all about?

Arabella
A little conspiracy. Very innocent.

Duchess (laughing)
That must be atrocious!

Arabella
You know that Félix still loves her!

Duchess
Who's that? My daughter?

Arabella
Doubtless. Duchess, do you grasp this Platonism—in perpetuity?

Duchess
What do you want, my sweet? Only that which doesn't exist lasts. That seems paradoxical, but it's true. So Mr. de Vandenesse sought the happiness of being near you. He found it! The problem is solved—and he reverts to the unknown. That's the algebra of love.

Arabella (rising)
Oh, that Touraine! I detest it. I will never be satisfied until that frightful country is reduced to the condition of Pompeii and I can have scraps of it on my mantelpiece.

Duchess (laughing and following her)
You are pretty as a picture when you are angry.

Arabella
If you knew how many times I've surprised Félix weeping, his lips glued to a letter from his dear valley, and—pardon my jealousy—but this letter—

Duchess
Well?

Arabella
I stole it from him.

Duchess
That's the only way to have what they don't want to give us.

Arabella
Near me, it's of the Countess that he thinks. He endures me, he loves her. Ah, Duchess, if she was not your daughter, I would hate her.

Duchess
Don't trouble yourself.

Arabella
Well! Frankly, that's what I am doing.

Duchess
The Countess is a fool to put her love in an envelope! What a provincial my daughter is. But, let's return to the duo of the conspiracy. Take your role.

Arabella
That's what it is, let's agree.

Duchess
I'm listening to you.

Arabella (lowering her voice a bit)
Excepting you, no one up to this point knows the truth about Mr. Félix and me.

Duchess (laughing)
You lower your eyes in a charming manner. Continue, then.

Arabella
To all the world, Mr. Vandenesse is only a friend.

Duchess
Yes, only that poor Mr. Cerny is compromised.

Arabella
Oh, he doesn't complain. That suffices for him.

Duchess
That's fair. Well!

Arabella
Here's my idea. I want to tear off a corner of the veil for the Chatelaine of Clocheguarde.

Duchess
I understand and, in truth, you will be rendering a great service to my son-in-law as well as my daughter herself. For, if we don't kill his love for her, his love will kill her. That is certain. And, in a final count, Henriette has more pride in her spirit than love in her heart. Learning that Mr. Vandenesse is just a man like all the others, she will positively scratch Saint Félix out of the calendar of Clocheguarde. That's very cleverly planned. Eh! Why now I think of it, is it for this that you are giving a ball?

Arabella
Yes, and that is also why I begged you to invite the Countess.

Duchess
Truly, I'm remorseful when I think that poor Henriette has put her head in the snare you've set for her. She was enchanted at the thought of falling unexpectedly in the midst of all her friends. She's going to spend a very disagreeable

evening.

Arabella (consoling her)
Why, it's in her interest and in the interest of Mr. de Vandenesse. Hasn't he just renounced his Embassy to London, always under the pretext of Touraine.

Duchess
Yes, yes. That's fair, and it's necessary to come up with a reason.

Arabella
And besides, I am going to make yet one more attempt on the heart of Mr. de Vandenesse. And if my love carries him away, I won't have any further recourse to the ruses of war. I promise you.

Duchess
Well! That's it! I am going to bring the Count and his wife.

(embracing Arabella)
But all the same, I am really fearful. All this is going to be very troublesome. Now here's an evening wasted by this little fool. Ah, if I didn't love her so much. Goodbye!

A Servant (announcing)
Mr. de Vandenesse.

Félix (entering and bowing)
Miladies.

Duchess
Mr. de Vandenesse, I am indeed your friend, and yet I am going to hand you over to Lady Arabella. Goodbye.

(low to Arabella) Till later.

(The Duchess leaves. When she has gone, Félix lowers himself onto a couch and remains a few moments without speaking.)

Arabella (after a silence)
Oh, it's incredible, what you are telling me.

Félix
Huh?

Arabella
Didn't you say something to me? (laughing) I thought—
You are remaining with us tonight?

Félix
Pardon, milady, but I came precisely to excuse myself—
my service near the king.

Arabella (laughing)
Oh, that's sacred!

(moment of silence)

Ah, indeed, look—decidedly—what's the matter with you, my dear Félix? On your face are all the mists of the Thames.

Félix
Indeed! I am sad—suffering—

Arabella
Would you like me to send after the doctor from Clocheguarde?

Félix
What doctor?

Arabella
I don't know.

(leaning on his shoulder) I'd like to get away. You must need solitude.

Félix
Solitude? Why?

Arabella
Why, to reread some letter—perhaps the one you were covering with burning kisses yesterday evening.

Félix
One more time, milady, I don't know what you mean.

Arabella
Was it by chance a letter from me?

Félix
Why, with no doubt!

Arabella (sitting next to him)
Eh, what! You reread those things? I didn't know they gave you such pleasure. Nothing's better, when tears fall from your eyes, than for them to be shed straight on to a paper always re-read and that ends by falling apart like an old coupon bond? It's a detestable custom, that you've got there, darling, a custom of an unhappy lover.

(smiling) Who gave it to you?

Félix
Coquette!

Arabella
You caught it in Touraine.

Félix
Arabella, stop the jests. I beg you, respect the purest of women.

Arabella
What then! But I respect her and I love her. I do love her. And her virtue, I revere it. Why, without this virtue you would be with her and what would become of my happiness? Happiness in my dress? In luxury? Ah, fie! Everybody can give themselves that sort of happiness and I detest vulgar felicities. Why, to possess a fine name, a princely fortune, and to forget all this, to love, with head held high, the idol one has chosen—and that nothing can make you betray—not even opinion. Ah, that's a true felicity! And it's assuredly to the morality of that good lady that I owe the happiness of tasting it.

Félix (with a bit less anger)
Arabella!

Arabella
After that, sir, if you are in a day of remorse, and if you love sermons, since Madame de Mortsauf isn't here, I will try to replace her. I will become preachy. But, you don't insist on that! Right?

(Félix gestures impotently)

Frankly, it will cost me. For I didn't study at Oxford or Edinburgh. My heart didn't take a degree. Poor me, I only know how to love. I am only your slave!

Félix (with love)
Hush, hush! I have no strength when I listen to you.

Arabella (smiling)
I know that quite well. And that is why I talk so much.

Félix (with love)
Keep talking.

Arabella (rising with a caressing voice)
Tell me. I want some information.

Félix (following her)
What is it?

Arabella (smiling)
Do you love me?

(Félix smiles)

My sultan smiled. It's the moment to present my request.

(caressingly) Vicomte, I would like to take a course in literature.

Félix
What's that mean?

Arabella
You have a model epistolary style. I'd like to study.

Félix
Arabella. I don't know—

Arabella (prayerfully)
Give me her letter! Hold on.

(touching his heart) It's there. It's taken my place.

Félix
Milady!

Arabella
Lend it to me for only five minutes. I will prove to you that she doesn't have common sense.

Félix (taking a step to leave)
Pardon, but I—

Arabella (holding him by his arm)
Look, I am not demanding that you yourself give me these precious lines. That would be a felonious act. Only, let me take them.

(Félix gently pushes her back.)

Arabella
Here, think about something else as you sometimes do, and during that time—

Félix
No, milady. I will never let you touch that letter.

Arabella (laughing)
You lie!

Félix
What do you mean?

Arabella
Yesterday, I took it from you.

Félix
Oh, that's unworthy.

Arabella (smiling)
No! It was clever.

Félix
That letter, milady, must be returned to me.

Arabella
That wouldn't make it worth taking.

Félix
Oh, you couldn't conceive the guilty thought—

Arabella
Pardon me, milord. The Countess will know everything. She will know that half your heart is in Touraine and the other half is in Paris.

Félix (enraged)
Well! Milady, you will be lying. For all my heart is down there.

Arabella
Ah, you are without pity for me, sir. Well, I will be without pity for her. The Countess will know, I swear it, that you've listened to the advice of the serpent—as you call me—and she will kick you out of her paradise.

Félix
Milady, I will put the Countess in shelter from your attempts. I will know how to prevent you from reaching her.

Arabella
Then, it's war. So be it. I accept it, Mr. de Vandenesse.

(aside) I will lose your love, but I will be avenged.

Félix (bowing)
Milady.

Emmeline (off)
Let me go, let me alone. I will announce myself.

Arabella (embracing Emmeline as she enters)
Eh! Good evening, my dear little girl. Well! All alone?

Emmeline
My father is here. He just met a deputy of the opposition in your antechamber and they are arguing improvements.

Arabella
That will be a long while and you did well to leave the session. Do you know, it's very sweet of you to come on ahead?

Emmeline
That wasn't without trouble. He didn't want to come at all. He wanted to take me to the theatre, but I cried so much—

Arabella (laughing)
You did well. you are going to set Mr. de Vandenesse at liberty. He who has an affair with the king and who felt obliged to keep me company.

Emmeline (gaily to Félix)
How serious you are! Aren't you going to say anything?

Félix (distracted)
I admire you. I'm happy to see this gaiety which makes you a thousand times more pretty than when you are sad.

Emmeline
A thousand times? I was really so ugly? (low to Arabella) Won't Mr. de Vandenesse be at the ball?

Arabella (looking at Félix)
Why, I fear not, my child. His service calls him.

Emmeline (pouting)
Ah, the king is very demanding.

(low) Make Félix promise to return.

Arabella
You cling to that idea?

Emmeline
Much.

(catching herself) He's such an excellent waltzer.

Arabella (low)
That's fine.

(going to Félix, aloud) Mr. de Vandenesse, don't trouble yourself. If you must attract the least reproach from His Majesty, better never to return.

Emmeline
Why, what are you saying?

Arabella (low)
Don't worry! In ten minutes he will be here.

Emmeline (low)
Really?

Félix (low to Arabella)
Milady, soon, I will ask for that letter again.

Arabella (low)
Soon, milord, I will have the new sorrow of refusing it to you.

Félix (low)
Arabella!

Arabella
Pardon! Hostilities have commenced.

(Arabella bows mockingly. Félix moves away. Chessel enters.)

Chessel (to Arabella)
Milady, I salute you.

Arabella
Mr. Chessel, take care of your infant. I will reclaim her soon. I must be mistress of the house for five minutes.

Emmeline (low to Arabella)
Well?

Arabella (low)
He'll be back.

Emmeline (low)
Bah!

Arabella (low)
From the moment you don't beg him.

Emmeline (low)
Ah, in that case.

(aloud) Goodbye, goodbye, Félix. Till tomorrow.

Félix
Soon!

Chessel (to Félix)
What? You're leaving?

Emmeline (aside with joy)
Milady was right. I will see him again. Still—

(Félix bows and leaves. Arabella goes into her apartment.)

Emmeline (gaily to her father)
How happy I am to be back in Paris!

Chessel
Really, and why?

Emmeline
I don't know. But at least I am much happier here than in Clocheguarde.

Chessel
Ah, indeed. How's it happen, Emmeline, that you are so friendly with Lady Arabella?

Emmeline
Ah, little daddy, it's a big secret.

Chessel
Really?

(laughing) Why then, if it's so big, you can give me half of it.

Emmeline (gaily)
You will swear not to tell anyone? Think, sir, it concerns the honor of a woman!

Chessel (dully)
I thought it was a question of Lady Arabella.

Emmeline (not understanding)
What? You want to know why I love Lady Dudley so much? Well, it's because I am so grateful to her.

Chessel
You?

Emmeline (lowering her voice)
Shh, lower! Yes, I am very grateful because it is she who advised Félix to accept this situation—in the king's cabinet—which keeps him in Paris. I am very grateful to her, also, for loving Mr. Cerny when she could have loved Félix.

Chessel
Why, what's that to you?

Emmeline
You don't know that I love him?

Chessel (starting)
You love him? You?

Emmeline
You hadn't guessed it?

Chessel
Yes. Yes, miss, a father guesses everything, always. You hear? (aside) What am I learning here?

Emmeline
Ah! You noticed?

Chessel
Your preference for Félix? By Jove, yes. Six months ago.

Emmeline
Six months? I loved him before he returned?

Chessel
Huh? Yes, no, I mean—

Emmeline
When Félix was down there in Clocheguarde, I was suffering so much; even the little girls noticed it, and I noticed that he loved Henriette.

Chessel
Ah, you did.

(aside) And there I was, fast asleep amidst all these dangers.

Emmeline
Father! What was the good of his loving Henriette, since she's married?

Chessel
Why, none, assuredly. Also, he really understood that, and

renounced her.

Emmeline
Ah, yes, it's true. Say, little daddy, when you see him, if you could tell him that I am a good little girl, very well behaved, and not very coquettish, who adores her father, that might be well.

Chessel
What?

Emmeline
Without seeming to, I beg you, tell him all that. It will call more attention to me and then I am very certain he will love me.

(she kisses him)

I'm going to run off, because if I were to stay longer, you would scold me. I'm going to find Lady Arabella.

Chessel
Ah, Emmeline? Listen—

Emmeline (hesitating to return)
It's not to scold me?

Chessel
No.

(Emmeline runs to her father.)

Chessel
Promise me not to say anything to Lady Arabella.

Emmeline

Oh, there's no danger of that. It's a secret between the two of us alone.

(she kisses him again.)

Chessel
Yes, yes.

Emmeline
The two of us alone.

(Emmeline leaves by the back.)

Chessel (very agitated)
Oh, I cannot hesitate. I must get Emmeline away. For from one minute to the next she might notice, and the poor little one would suffer too much if she had to renounce her hopes again. We will leave. We'll return to Touraine. As for Félix, well, as the innocent child herself said, perhaps one day—(with chagrin)

And when I think that for such a long while I didn't see a thing. I who have such good eyes for seeing things that are no concern of mine. Ah, a daughter ought never to lose her mother.

Count (entering with the Duchess)
Come on, it's impossible—and I cannot believe it.

Duchess
It's a fact. Here, why not ask Mr. Chessel?

Chessel
Huh? What's it about?

Duchess
About a little scandal freshly blooming.

Chessel
I don't know.

Duchess
Well! It seems that Mr. de Vandenesse is the lover of Lady Arabella.

Chessel
Speak lower, mercy.

Duchess
Why? The walls know it.

Count
Can you see this little Félix with his bending airs— (stooping)

Duchess
Exactly. From bending, one falls to stooping.

Count (laughing)
Ah, ah, ah! And this husband who is in India!

Duchess
My God, yes. He's in India. Husbands are all there, more or less. Ah, indeed. They are never able to know. My dear Mr. Chessel, you aren't saying anything, you aren't laughing. When you come to the home of an Englishwoman, do you think yourself obliged to have the spleen?

Chessel
Excuse me, Duchess.

Count
You'd say my friend Chessel has some worries.

Duchess
Is he ill?

Chessel
Why, a little, Duchess. Enough even to be obliged to retire, if my little Emmeline will permit it.

Duchess
Well, go ask her permission. She is in the greenhouse, I believe. There are people already. My daughter and Mr. de Vandenesse that we brought—

Chessel
I thank you again. I'm going to rejoin Emmeline. Good-bye, Count.

(Chessel leaves.)

Duchess (laughing)
Ah, ah, ah! My friend Chessel is so discomfited by gaiety. Up until now I thought that only my son-in-law was tiresome.

Count (vexed)
Duchess!

Duchess
Ah, we're not telling truths. Here's company.

(Félix and Henriette enter from the back.)

Félix (uneasy) I—

(aside) The Duchess with the Count. It's a trap, a betrayal.

Henriette (to Count)
My friend, Lady Dudley sent us looking for you.

Duchess
I am going to make her learn patience.

(aside) Let's go tell her the fire is in the powder.

(low to Count) I confide our patient to you.

(pointing to Félix) Return him to me cured of Arabella.

Count
Don't worry. I am going to have a consultation with my wife.

Duchess
That's an excellent idea!

Count
She has a great empire over him.

(The Count goes off with the Duchess. They talk low, then the Duchess disappears.)

Henriette (seated at the left)
What did Lady Arabella say to you just now?

Félix
Jealous!

Henriette
Yes, jealous of this share of affection I've been able to keep without crime, of this fraternal love that I thought

impossible and in which you've made me believe. And my letter? Did you re-read it often? And have you followed the advice that I gave you?

Félix
Yes, darling Henriette! And believe me, although one may not tell you—

Henriette
What?

Count (coming quietly between them)
Can one enter?

(Félix rises excitedly)

I distract you? You were perhaps paying court to my wife?

Félix
Count!

Count
Oh, damn, you are a seducer. I can tell. I know about your pranks.

Félix (with terror)
Sir!

Count (looking behind him)
Don't worry, we are alone. And then, besides, it's not a mystery. Everybody's talking about it.

Félix
I don't know what you mean.

Count
Eh! Don't be so discreet, it's too late. But as we are your friends, we are going, if you please, to preach you a sermon in three parts.

Félix (aside)
Oh, my God! Now that's what I was afraid of!

Count
If you will permit me, my dear friend, I will tell you that you are entered into a deplorable path.

Félix
Mercy.

Count
But no, my dear friend, I won't be quiet. One is a friend or one is not. This liaison compromises your future and it would be faint-hearted not to scold you and not to yell danger when you are marching towards an abyss. If at least this woman were free! Or if she had only a sick husband, a poor devil like me, you would see a way out of that, a possible marriage in the future. But, Lord Dudley's in very good health.

Henriette
Lord Dudley! So that's it?

Count
Lady Arabella, doubtless. Didn't I tell you?

Félix (overwhelmed, aside)
I am lost!

Count
And besides, who is to say that the man you are intriguing

won't come one day to ask for an account of the blot placed on his name? Who says this romantic novel you opened in some boudoir won't close in the depths of some solitary forest?

Henriette (with a cry)
Ah!

Count
But, I'm mad. I'm talking, talking. I will give myself a sore throat. I leave you to Henriette. Finish by converting him.

(gaily giving Félix his hand) As to the rest, my dear friend, if I've given you advice for the future, receive my compliments for the past. Lady Arabella is charming, isn't she, Henriette?

Henriette
Yes, indeed.

Count
You did well to love her yesterday, but you're wrong to love her today, and you would be unforgivable if you love her tomorrow. Think about it, believe me, arrange your affairs, liquidate this love, bankrupt it.

(Félix gestures)

(laughing) Bye, bye.

(The Count goes out. After a moment of silence, Félix approaches Henriette.)

Félix
Henriette, in heaven's name, don't condemn me without

hearing me.

Henriette (forcing a smile)
Why do you justify yourself? You are forgivable, Félix, for having forgotten me. It's I who am not for having believed your words a second time. Wasn't this the height of egoism, to ask you to sacrifice to the shade of happiness, apparently great felicities, since to taste them, there are women who sacrifice the sacred title of spouse and mother?

Félix
Why, that woman. I don't love her. I never loved her!

Henriette (coldly)
Félix, give me back that letter that I wrote you.

(severely) I want it, I want it!

Félix (embarrassed)
Mercy!

Henriette (bitterly)
Did you give it to Lady Arabella?

Arabella (coming in)
No, Madame, it was I who took it.

Félix (enraged)
Arabella!

Arabella
Oh, don't get carried away, milord. I'm coming to your aid. I'm coming to plead your case.

Félix
Milady!

Arabella
Eh, what? Madame, this sweet little letter, a bit long perhaps for a "billet-doux," this sweet little letter is the only pledge that your virtuous love consented to give, and you want it back? This repentance before sinning, it's too soon.

Félix
Shut up! Shut up!

Henriette
No, no, let Madame speak. That will be my punishment.

Arabella
What, Madame? You want to have everything, the respect of the world, the esteem of your husband, the affection of your child, and the love—of your lover—when just one of those goodies would suffice for the happiness of a woman?

Félix (exploding)
One more time, milady!

Arabella
Be careful, they might hear you.

(to Henriette) To give one's heart, Madame, or rather to refuse it—but to refuse it while moralizing in four illegible pages—ah—why, it's contrary to the law of nations.

Félix
Oh, that's too many insults. Madame, give me that letter.

Arabella
I've refused it to you twice, sir. No, I am dreaming of keeping this letter in a sumptuous box, supported by two cupids, or rather, no, by two angels.

Henriette (aside, with humiliation)
Oh!

Arabella
Madame regrets her amours?

Henriette (aside)
Oh, I am well punished.

Arabella
I will often place before the eyes of Mr. de Vandenesse these proofs of fraternal love. I will make him read the strict commandments and it's I who will force him, Madame, to return to your husband and to your child the share of the affection of which he robbed them.

Henriette
Madame, I thank heaven for putting me at your mercy. I accept your outrages as the first expiation of my sin. I have been guilty. I have been criminal. Yes, criminal, for it is a crime to isolate oneself in the bosom of the family, to be alone with memories that don't belong to the whole family. It's a crime, also, to marry one's soul secretly, and to bow one's head to receive a spouse's kisses on your hair, while keeping a pure face for one's lover.

(forcefully) It's a crime to forge a future while leaning on the dead!

(Henriette falls exhausted into a chair. Félix rushes toward her.)

Félix
Henriette!

Henriette
Sir, I am the Countess de Mortsauf.

Félix (raging)
Arabella!

(Music is heard.)

Arabella (with pride, returning the letter to Félix)
Sir, I return your heart to you.

(to Henriette, with a smile) Madame, I give him to you.

(Arabella leaves with head held high.)

Henriette (aside, weeping)
My God! My God! This is too much humiliation.

Félix
Henriette!

Henriette
Henriette no longer exists, sir. You've killed her.

(aside) Oh, I feel it keenly. I am dying!

CURTAIN

ACT V

Henriette's room. To the right a door. Near it a chimney with a mirror. To the left of the chimney, a chaise lounge in which Henriette is sitting. Emmeline is seated to her right on a small chair. To the right a round table at which the Count and Chessel are seated. At the back a bay window on each side of a door. A lamp lit on the table.

Henriette is stretched out before the fire. She is drowsy. Emmeline is asleep in her chair at Henriette's foot. The Count and Chessel are speaking low at the table.

Chessel
Ah, Emmeline's asleep. She hasn't shut her eyes in three days and her strength has betrayed her.

Count
What do you think? She pretends she feels better when she gets up! All the same, she gets a little rest, I think.

Chessel (deploring)
Yes, opium puts her sorrows to sleep.

Count
That poor child! But still, she—she's young, while as for me! Ah, my friend! I feel it keenly. I am lost.

Chessel (sitting down, impatiently, but low)
Count, it's not you who are lost. It's the Countess.

Count
And can you understand this bullheadedness? There's nothing to say. She hasn't eaten for a month.

Chessel
It's a month since she's been able to eat, you mean?

Count (placing his head in his hands)
Oh, I feel my head is coming apart. There are moments where I have no awareness of anything. It seems to me I am going mad with this deathly atmosphere in this room. If one could open it a little—

Chessel (containing him)
You know that the doctor recommended heat.

Count
Ah, the doctors are asses.

(Chessel shrugs his shoulders)

Why are you shrugging your shoulders? You are, indeed, always the same. You have no pity for me.

Chessel
At the moment it is not a question of you or me.

Chessel
I know that as well as you, by Jove! Do you think I don't know it?

Chessel
Silence. Mercy.

Count
Ah, indeed! And Madeleine? Where is she? Is she sleeping?

Chessel
She was asleep in her mother's arms. Then I took her to her bed.

Count
Sick people are sometimes demanding. Because they never sleep, they think others no longer need to sleep. When the Château becomes a hospital that will remedy a lot.

Chessel (coldly)
Count, if you will go get some rest, I will watch.

Count
Oh, you will watch, you will watch. You aren't made of iron either.

Chessel
Look, would you leave her alone?

Count
Alone? It seems to me I am not hard enough, not egoist enough for that.

Chessel
Them, watch with me.

Count
Well, it seems to me that's what I am doing.

Chessel (aside)
Oh, what a man!

Count
That Duchess de Lenoncourt! See if she's coming? We wrote her that her daughter was ill. If she was here, it would be better for everybody. God be thanked! She's used to staying up all night. As for her, she's up enough for the ball.

Chessel
It's only yesterday that the letter was sent to Madame de Lenoncourt, you know.

Count
Yes, that's true. Another of Henriette's ideas.

Chessel
She didn't want to worry her mother until the last possible moment.

Count
Oh, with that the Duchess is a really tender mother? I don't know of any egoist with such strength.

Chessel (between his teeth)
Indeed, he doesn't know himself.

Count
What? What are your saying? I'm an egoist? Me?

Chessel
Eh, yes, damnation! Because you annoy me in the end with your perpetual complaining. Am I talking about my sufferings since that evening when I discovered in my child's heart a love that perhaps may kill her, too, some day?

Count
You see plainly that you are speaking of me!

Chessel
Ought one to think of one's own sorrows in the presence of this poor woman who has, perhaps, not two hours to live.

Count
Well, is that my fault?

Chessel
A little, Count, for you didn't give to this angel (emphasizing) all the happiness she deserved.

Count
No, I didn't, but it's a crying injustice to blame me—. Ask Henriette herself if—

Chessel
Yes, let's wake her for that?

Count (raising his voice a bit)
Eh, damn! I didn't tell you to wake her.

Chessel
Still, that's what's going to happen if you yell like that.

Count (very low)
I'm not yelling. That's horrible, to tell me that I—Why, if I thought that, I'd blow my brains out. Yes, sir. Very bad of you.

(As the Count says this, he is preparing a glass of sugared water.)

Chessel
Would you like some orange flavoring?

Count (putting down the glass without drinking)
You are impertinent!

Chessel (half laughing)
It seems you don't want to blow your brains out.

(Manette tiptoes in quietly.)

Manette (low to Count)
Count, Germain has been to the post. The carriage hasn't yet arrived. Mr. Félix probably won't come today.

(leaves)

Chessel (to Count)
Mr. Félix?

Count
Well, yes. I wrote him, wrote to him to come. I thought that his presence would be agreeable to this poor Henriette and by parentheses I told him everything on the subject of Emmeline.

Chessel
What?

Count
You see, I am thinking only of myself.

Chessel
So, Mr. de Vandenesse is going to come?

Count
I hope so, for Henriette wants him. Here, the poor child, as you see, made herself once more beautiful to receive him. They had to put flowers in the vases the way she used to put them herself, another fantasy of the ill.

Manette (returning)
Sir, here's Doctor Origet.

Count
The Doctor!

(Chessel and the Count go to the Doctor as he enters. They don't speak. The Doctor goes quietly to Henriette, looks at her, takes her pulse, and shakes his head, sighing.)

Chessel
Well, sir?

Doctor (low voice)
Soon the opium will have no more effect. The Countess is going to wake up. Come, come, I cannot speak to you here.

Count (aside)
O my God! My God! What a night!

Doctor
Silence!

(The Doctor, Chessel, and the Count leave. Emmeline is still asleep. Henriette slowly raises her head and watches them leave.)

Henriette
The Doctor! They are there.

(as if struck by an idea) Ah, it's over.

(Henriette turns and notices Emmeline.)

Emmeline (dreaming)
There were sunflowers! I suffered a lot, but I am happy.
Félix! I love you!

(Henriette makes an abrupt movement. Emmeline wakes
up with a start.)

Emmeline
Ah! I was drowsy.

(after a silence) Why, how you are staring at me!

Henriette (in a strange tone)
Do I frighten you?

Emmeline (frightened, forcing a smile)
No, why, no.

Henriette (playing with Emmeline's hair, to herself, re-
  gretfully)
Eighteen! A long future, and a love that is permitted.

Emmeline
What's the matter with you?

Henriette (keeping a fixed look)
Nothing.

Emmeline
Are you worse?

Henriette
Why, no.

Emmeline (tearfully)
Henriette, speak to me! Have I done something? Speak.
Are you mad at me? Why are you crying?

Henriette
Am I crying?

Emmeline
Why, yes.

(Emmeline goes to Henriette and dries her eyes. Henriette
pushes her gently away.)

Henriette
Emmeline, do you love him?

Emmeline (troubled)
Who's that?

Henriette
Félix?

Emmeline
Why, no. I assure you.

Henriette (in a dry tone)
You said so, just now, in your sleep.

Emmeline
Why, I—

(Emmeline lowers her eyes. Henriette leans over to her.)

And him? He loves you too, doubtless?

Emmeline (excitedly with a sort of joy)
No, no. I swear to you, on my mother.

Henriette (with a ray of joy)
Ah!

Emmeline (with pity)
Poor Henriette.

Henriette (after a sort of distracted silence)
Say, my child, Lady Arabella left for England, right?

Emmeline
Yes, yes.

Henriette
You swear it to me?

Emmeline
I swear it.

Henriette (listening suddenly)
Ah, my God!

Emmeline
What's wrong?

Henriette (placing her hand on her heart)
Don't you feel anything there? You, don't you hear any-thing—in your heart?

Emmeline (uneasy)
Henriette!

Henriette (aside in a triumphant tone)
She doesn't love him more than me!

(taking Emmeline and pointing to the door at the left)
Here, look. He's here, he's coming!

(Félix enters and stops.)

Emmeline (with a choked cry)
Félix!

(Emmeline rises and goes to Félix who shakes her hand. Then Emmeline leaves without saying a word. Henriette takes a mirror and furtively arranges her hair. Félix goes to her and sits in the seat Emmeline left.)

Henriette
Hello, Vicomte.

Félix (aside)
My God! What a change.

Henriette (with a smile)
Ah, why did I want you so much? I was a mad woman. As for me, I want to live in your memory like an eternal lily. I want to carry off all your illnesses.

Félix (hiding his emotions)
Henriette.

Henriette
I am really ugly, aren't I? Still, I got all dressed up for you, Félix.

Félix
My friend!

(Henriette rises with effort and draws Félix far from the lamp, towards the window.)

Henriette
Wait here. You won't be able to see me as well. Come near this window, where we leaned so often together. Hearts drowned in dreams that we told each other endlessly. You remember the day I said to you: "The mother of a family remains, and will remain forever, impassive, radiant, protected by her children, until her last petal falls with the last rosy tear"?

Félix
Yes, I remember.

Henriette (with the beginning of delirium)
Well, I lied! I was lying. Her last tear, Félix, is a tear of regret for love. But, don't be desolate, it's not time yet. And already, I'm feeling better. Here you are. I will be reborn under your glances. I will become beautiful again! I am young, I am not going to die yet. They don't know what they're talking about.

(after a silence) Listen, I've made some plans. We are going to live in Italy.

Félix (aside)
My God!

Henriette
Huh?

Félix
Why, then you no longer love our dear valley?

Henriette
It's sepulchral to me without you—without you. And then, it gets cold here, whereas, down there, that beautiful sun will restore my life. The lily bent down today will proudly raise up her head. I will ride a horse like her. I will be crazy like her. I will love like her.

Félix
Henriette! Darling Henriette.

Henriette (whose delirium increases bit by bit)
No, you see, I've had enough of life's deceptions. Everything in my life has been a lie and an imposture. I buried my love alive in my heart, but it's not dead, it's being born again. It lives, it exists! Oh, no, no, I won't die! I don't want to die. Before knowing death's secrets, I intend to know life's secrets.

Félix (aside)
Oh, this is horrible!

(At this moment the Angelus can be heard in the distance. Henriette listens at first without comprehending, then slowly comes to herself.)

Henriette (with shame)
Oh, my God! My God! Pardon me.

Félix
Henriette!

Henriette (going to the chaise lounge)
It's no longer love I ask of you, but prayers.

(sinks down)

Félix (choked by tears)
Henriette! Henriette!

Count (rushing in)
What's wrong? What's wrong?

Henriette
Nothing. Nothing yet, Count! God I hope will give me time and strength to accuse myself before you.

(she kneels)

Count (trying to raise her)
Henriette!

Henriette
Sir, although I may have lived as a virtuous spouse according to human laws, guilty thoughts often crossed my heart. I had, for a long while, a lively friendship that no one, not even the man who was the object of it, knew in its entirety. But, I swear to you, Count, I have nothing more to tell a priest who I am awaiting. Deign to absolve me like him!

Count (raising her in his arms)
Henriette! Henriette! Do you want to kill me?

Henriette (in an increasingly weak voice)
Do you forgive me?

Count (in tears)
Poor angel! Will you forgive me?

Henriette
Oh, my friend, don't accuse yourself. That would be to condemn my mother, and despite the past, I bless you both, you and my mother. Emmeline.

(Emmeline has been standing in the doorway)

Approach, my child.

(to Félix) Félix, do you swear to execute the last wishes of your friend?

Félix
I swear it.

Henriette (to Emmeline)
And you?

(Emmeline nods, weeping. Henriette joins the hands of Félix and Emmeline.)

Henriette
Félix, love her well. And you, Emmeline, watch over my child! My strength abandons me. My sight is troubled, and yet—(pointing to the mirror in a sort of delirium) What's that light? That silver cross that marches there? (calmly) Ah, yes, I know. I am going to see God! Like you said, Madeleine! But you—(with tears) I won't ever see you any more except on high, up there.

CURTAIN

www.ingramcontent.com/pod-product-compliance
Lightning Source LLC
La Vergne TN
LVHW091258080426
835510LV00007B/312